COMMON SENSE PARENTING

COMMON SENSE
PARENTING

A proven, step-by-step guide for raising responsible kids and building happy families

Ray Burke, Ph.D.
Ron Herron

PENTAGON PRESS

COMMON SENSE PARENTING

First published in India by

by THIRD EYE
An Imprint of

PENTAGON PRESS
206, Peacock Lane, Shahpur Jat,
New Delhi-110049
Phones: 011-64706243, 26491568
Telefax: 011-26490600
email: rajan@pentagon-press.com
website: www.pentagon-press.com

PUBLISHED BY ARRANGEMENT WITH
BT PRESS, FATHER FLANAGAN'S BOY'S HOME,
BOYS TOWN, NEBRASKA, USA

First published: 2005
Reprinted: 2006, 2009

ISBN 978-81-8274-970-2

Printed by New Elegant Printers, New Delhi.

Acknowledgments

This book would not have been possible without the generous work of many helping hands along the way. A huge thanks goes to all of the Boys Town staff, past and present, who have contributed to the development of the ideas we share on the following pages. Too numerous to mention individually, their personal contributions have laid the foundation for Common Sense Parenting.

A special thanks goes to all of the parents who have participated in the program over the years; to the Common Sense Parenting staff for their creative ideas and tireless work; and to the Boys Town Press for their detailed editing and suggestions.

Table of Contents

Introduction

You have a job to do – the most important job of your life. You're a parent. Some people say it doesn't pay well. The benefits aren't always the greatest. The hours are lousy. And the work is never-ending.

But oh, what a wonderful job it is. Parents sometimes look at us with more than a little skepticism when we tell them that parenthood is one of the richest and most satisfying experiences in life. After all, who enjoys wiping runny noses, rousting grouchy kids out of bed to get ready for school, taxiing them here and there, listening to griping about unfairness and yucky vegetables, arguing and complaining and nasty moods. But that's just the surface stuff; there's a lot more to the whole package of being a parent. What really matters are the bonds you create, the relationships and values of your family that you hand down for generations to come.

Like most jobs, parenting involves lots of on-the-job training. Unfortunately, with no actual training program or supervisor, parents are faced with many situations they don't know how to handle. They may respond instinctively and afterwards wonder if they did the right thing. They may lack self-confidence in their parenting abilities. Sometimes things go well; sometimes they don't.

All parents occasionally need some help and advice when they are having a tough time with their kids. All parents occasionally doubt their effectiveness. That's why we wrote this book. Parenting isn't easy; we know that. We, at Boys Town, have been parents to more than 17,000 young people. That's a bunch of kids! What we have learned adds up to a practical method that can help all parents. That's the method we have taught thousands of parents through our Common Sense Parenting® classes.

What makes Common Sense Parenting work so well? We emphasize two things: the "head" and the "heart." The "head" means using a logical, practical method of teaching your children; in other words using skills to change your kids' behavior. The "heart" means having unconditional love for your children. One without the other will not work. Put them both together and you have a powerful combination.

This book offers you a blueprint for parenting that has been effective with families just like yours. Whether you are a parent who wishes to "brush up" on your parenting skills, or an excited "rookie" with your first child, or an exasperated parent with rebellious or difficult children, this book can help you.

We all know that there are no such creatures as perfect parents or perfect kids. We live in a sometimes messy, imperfect world and we're going to make mistakes, no matter how hard we try. It's also true that no book, class, or training program alone can solve all of a family's problems. It would be foolish to make such a guarantee. Our lives are too complex to have exact answers for everything. However, the skills you learn in Common Sense Parenting – the logical techniques and foundations for discipline – give you a plan for making fewer mistakes and doing a better job in the future. Research studies done on the skills we teach are very positive. Parents report that they feel more satisfied and effective in their roles as parents and that their children have fewer behavior problems.

You are your children's first and most important teacher. No one should have a greater impact on your kids' lives than you. That means you have to bring to the task all the love, patience, and energy you can muster. Through all of this, you will find that parenting is the most exciting challenge you will ever face. Make the most of it.

One last thing. All of the skills in this book rely on one crucial element of parenting. That element is spending time with your kids. You can only teach them if you're with them. It's as simple as that. You can enjoy the richness of family only if you spend time together. It's absolutely, positively a must. It is the glue that holds a family together.

Good luck. You're on an exciting path toward becoming a better parent. Your love and the skills you learn in Common Sense Parenting are going to make a positive difference in your family. Love your children even when they least deserve it. Then, teach them the proper way to behave. This book gives you the teaching tools to help your kids. Good parenting relies on the combination of those skills and your love. Make the most of the opportunities you have with your children.

Teach them well.

How to Use This Book

Parents are some of the busiest people we know. They usually juggle several schedules, have an enormous list of things to get done each day, and have little time for "extras" such as reading this book. With that in mind, we wrote this book in short chapters so that you could "digest" a little information without taking up a lot of your time.

Each chapter outlines a parenting skill and gives examples of how to use that skill with your children in a variety of situations. We encourage you to practice and memorize the steps to each skill and use them frequently. Feel free to pick up this book any time you experience some rough spots and need a reminder of how to handle a specific problem.

We fully realize that there is no "perfect" answer to the problems parents face. Each situation, each parent, and each child is unique. For that reason, we offer you practical guidelines and suggestions that can easily be adapted into your own "style" of interacting with your children. We also offer teaching methods that you should learn and use until they become second-nature. As you use these skills, you should expect positive behavior changes in your children.

The techniques listed in this book are unique, also. Many books about child care deal with a specific age group of children. Our techniques can be used with children from ages 6 to 16, applied with your common sense and logic to fit the age and developmental level of your children. In this way, the teaching skills described become valuable tools to help you build on the strengths and improve the weaknesses in each of your kids.

Just one note about the change process. Change takes time. The behaviors your children now display are a result of all the learning they have experienced in their lives. Learning new behaviors won't occur overnight. Things often get worse before they get better. It's much like remodeling a house. You live with a lot of dust and dirt before you ever have things the way you want them. At times, you may feel like throwing up your hands and saying "What's the use?" We encourage you not to do that. Just like with remodeling, you can complete the task at hand through patience, hard work, and perseverance.

Expect some pitfalls. Understand that it takes time and effort. Learn to look at each improvement as a step in the right direction. Pat yourself on the back when you conquer a problem with one of your kids. The moments of self-doubt you experience will eventually be replaced with a renewed confidence in your parenting abilities. What's more, you will feel a positive sense of direction in how you teach your children.

There are no magical cures for the problems parents face. But the skills in this book have helped thousands of parents deal with and prevent the situations that trouble many families. We hope you, like so many other parents, find these skills to be practical, useful, and beneficial.

Chapter 1

Punishment vs. Teaching

Discipline is commonly misunderstood. As parents, we may each take a different approach to discipline. This may include punishment, correction, and/or guidance. Before we discuss our approach to discipline, please take a moment to answer the following questions about the way you deal with your children and their misbehaviors.

1. Do you find yourself arguing with your kids about their behavior?
2. Do you feel like all you do is correct your kids?
3. Do you often respond with a big punishment for a relatively minor misbehavior?
4. Do you use threats that you won't or can't carry out?
5. Do you find yourself saying things to your child that you later regret?
6. Do you repeat the same instructions to your kids over and over?
7. Do you often give in to your child's demands because you feel it's not worth the hassle to deal with him or her?
8. Do you find that the more you punish, the more your child misbehaves?
9. Do you resort to physical punishment because you think nothing else works?

If you answered "Yes" to some of these questions, there is a good chance you are relying on punishment. If so, you're not alone. Most parents, as a recent survey on parenting indicated, use punitive or unpleasant responses when their kids misbehave. This means parents yell, scold, call their kids names, or use physical punishment. The use of punishment is commonplace. And, we won't try to convince you that punishment doesn't work. It does. But, that doesn't mean parents should use it; punishment is not the best way to discipline children.

Inappropriate Punishment

We define inappropriate punishment as something that is harsh and unreasonable, violent and harmful. Corporal punishment such as hitting, slapping, or punching hurts children, emotionally as well as physically.

Inappropriate punishments also include such behaviors as screaming, belittling, ridiculing, and isolating. The key ingredient to all inappropriate punishment is the harm it causes to a child's development.

Then why do parents use inappropriate punishment so often?

First of all, punishment seems to get an immediate change in behavior. Sometimes, it gives short-term results that seem effective. The first few times we yelled at the kids, they got quiet. Yelling has to work, right? Wrong. In the short run, inappropriate punishment can get what we want, but over time, it results in all sorts of problems for us and our children.

A second reason parents use inappropriate punishment is that they are not sure of what else to do in those situations. They are angry and frustrated and react to what their child said or did – almost like it was automatic. Hitting, yelling, and spanking are common punishments when parents react without thinking.

The third reason probably has been felt by all parents at one time or another – the fear of losing their authority. Parents have a fear that if they aren't tough enough, their kids will run all over them, and the kids will be in control, not the parents. When parents feel the need to become tougher – to let the kids know "they really mean business" – they often resort to using inappropriate punishment.

The last reason parents use inappropriate punishment is because no one taught them any other way. They learned from the models set for them; they learned from their parents. There's nothing wrong with this; we all learned from our parents. But, if a person's parents used inappropriate punishment, it is likely that he or she will use similar types of punishment.

Here are two examples of inappropriate punishment:

Mahesh is playing with the TV video game. Jai doesn't want to wait his turn, so he walks up and unplugs the game. Mahesh hits him with a Ping-Pong paddle. Mom hears what's going on, comes in, lifts Mahesh up, shakes him, and says, "Don't hit your brother!"

Priti draws a picture on the living room wall with a red crayon. She finds Mom, shows her the picture, and asks her if she likes it. Mom spanks Priti and sends her to her room for an hour.

Negative Effects of Inappropriate Punishment

If you use inappropriate punishment, there's a good chance that your kids will respond with a lot of unpleasant behavior such as yelling, swearing, or mumbling under their breath and walking away. They probably don't feel very good about the punishment you used – and neither do you. It's also likely that your kids won't learn what they should do to avoid trouble in the future.

Inappropriate punishment affects the way children think about themselves. They don't feel good about themselves after being put down, yelled at, hit, or slapped.

Punishment often results in revenge. Children want to get back at the person who punished them.

Punishment damages relationships between parents and their children. Children may want to avoid their parents altogether.

Punishment can have a snowball effect. If one punishment

doesn't work, parents often try a harsher one; a parent's response can escalate from requests to commands, to yelling, to hitting. Life becomes a constant battle between parents and kids.

Appropriate Teaching

The focus of this entire book is to show you how to teach your children in a better way, without having to resort to the use of inappropriate punishment. In Common Sense Parenting, we use what we call "appropriate teaching." All of the skills outlined in this book provide the foundation for appropriate teaching to take place.

Appropriate teaching provides a positive and effective approach to problem behavior. Appropriate teaching is:

Specific – you let your children know exactly what they do right or wrong.

Responsive – you help your children understand the relationship between what they do and what happens as a result of their actions.

Concrete – you give your children clear examples of how to improve in the future.

Positive – you help your children learn self-discipline (to be in control of their actions and expressions of emotion).

Interactive – you give your children a chance to show what they have learned. You are an active part of the learning process. You and your children work together toward a common goal.

Informative – you become the teacher, the coach, as you give information that helps your children learn to solve problems.

In other words, appropriate teaching helps build self-confidence, teaches kids to get along well with others, and gives them the skills to make their own decisions.

Appropriate teaching helps children learn self-discipline. And, they are much more likely to learn when they are treated with affection and pleasantness rather than anger and physical punishment. It provides a positive framework for learning to take place.

Appropriate teaching tells kids what they did right and why they should continue it, or what they did wrong and how to correct it. If you are pleasant, firm, consistent, and able to give clear messages, you will be teaching effectively.

Here are two examples of appropriate teaching.

Sushila and her friend are walking into the living room and talking about the new girl in school. Sushila's mom overhears Sushila tell her friend that they shouldn't play with the new girl anymore because she doesn't wear neat clothes. Her mom asks the girls to sit down and they talk about how clothes shouldn't determine how someone feels about another person. Mom says that it is what's inside a person that is important, not what's on the outside. The girls agree to ask the new girl over after school.

Dad tells Tushar that he can't go outside to shoot baskets because Tushar has homework to finish. Tushar gets angry, stomps his feet, and complains how unfair his father is. Dad tells Tushar that they need to talk about Tushar's behavior. First, Tushar needs to calm down and stop yelling. Moments later, after Tushar has settled down, Dad explains to Tushar that he needs to learn how to accept "No" for an answer.

Summary

We hope you have a general understanding of the differences between inappropriate punishment and appropriate teaching. While both may have an immediate effect on children's behavior, appropriate teaching has greater potential for long-term benefits. This book provides you with positive alternatives to inappropriate punishment.

Appropriate teaching relies on being clear and specific, and understanding the relationships between behaviors and their consequences. We'll talk more about these crucial elements in future chapters.

Notes

Chapter 2

Clear Messages

"You've got a lousy attitude!"

"Shape up, Saroj. Stop being so naughty."

"You were a good boy at the store."

"Remember to be nice to your teacher today."

These are common statements made by parents. But, do children really understand what their parents mean? Probably not. We must remember that most children are concrete thinkers; they don't grasp the full meaning of words that are abstract or vague.

As teachers for our children, we have to be clear in our communication with them. Terms like "disrespectful," "naughty," "irresponsible," etc., are far from clear, concrete descriptions. For kids, this can be confusing and frustrating.

A clear message when describing a "lousy attitude" might be, "You walked away from me when I asked you to do something, and mumbled 'Get off my back.'" Or a clear alternative to telling to your son that he was a "nice boy at the store" would be, "You sat quietly in the cart and helped me arrange the groceries. That was nice." This gives the child specific information. One of our goals as parents is to **give our kids messages they can understand.**

Giving clear messages is one key to appropriate teaching. Parents need to specifically tell their children what needs to be done and how to do it. They need to clearly let their children know when they've done well and also need to clearly let them know when they've misbehaved. Finally, parents need to teach their children how to think for themselves and solve problems.

This means parents must be specific; they have to focus on what their children are doing or saying, and accurately describe their children's behaviors.

Everyone has a general idea of what behaviors are, but to make sure we're on the same wavelength, let's take a look at a specific definition that can help you give clear messages.

What Is Behavior?

Have you ever listened to a sporting event on the radio? If you have, you know that a good sports announcer can help you visualize what is happening by giving vivid descriptions. You can see every play in your mind. The sportscaster is giving a verbal replay of the action taking place. We need to be just as clear with our kids when we describe their behavior.

But what exactly is behavior? Behavior is what people do or say – in other words, behavior is anything a person does that can be seen, heard, or measured. Here are some specific descriptions of behavior:

"My daughter talks on the phone for one hour at a time."

"When I ask my son to do something, he rolls his eyes and walks away."

"When my kids come home from school, they put their books away and ask if there's anything that needs to be done around the house."

"When I tell my daughter her jeans are too tight, she whines and screams and asks me why I'm always on her back."

"My son helps me put away the dishes, then rinses the sink and sweeps the kitchen floor."

When you read these sentences, you get a clear picture of what the children are doing. When you teach your children, describing their behavior lets them know what they've done well or what they need to change.

It is easy to understand what we mean by a person's actions that can be seen or heard. But parents often ask, "What does it mean to 'measure' behavior?" Think of it this way: Lying on the couch is a behavior; it's something a person does. You can measure **how long** your son lies on the couch by the amount of time that goes by. You can also measure **how often** he lies on the couch by putting a check mark on the calendar every time he does it. Measuring how often or how long some behavior occurs is another way of clearly describing behavior.

Giving Clear Messages

In order to give clear messages, you must first watch what your child does or says. Then, clearly and specifically tell your child what was done correctly or incorrectly. It's like giving an instant replay of their behavior. Use words that you know your child will understand. For younger children, use short sentences and easily understood words. As they get older, adjust your language to fit their age and level of understanding.

When giving clear messages, it will help to describe some of the following:

Who is involved? Who is being praised? Whose behavior is being corrected?

What just happened? What was done well? What needs to be improved or changed?

When did the behavior happen?

Where did the behavior occur?

How you give messages is also very important. Here are several points that will help you convey clear messages to your children:

Have your child look at you. It's more likely that your child will hear what you say and follow through on any requests. Our experience has taught us that eye contact is a key to giving and receiving clear messages.

Look at your child. This allows you to see your child's reaction to what you say. Give your child your full attention. When both of you are looking at each other, it helps improve communication.

Use a voice tone that fits the situation. Your voice should be firm when giving correction, friendly and enthusiastic when giving compliments.

Eliminate as many distractions as possible. Try to find a quiet area where you can talk to your child.

Try to position yourself so that you are at eye level with your child. Avoid intimidating your child by standing over him or her.

Let's compare vague descriptions of kids' behavior with specific descriptions of the same situation.

Vague – "Bhaskar, why can't you act your age when company comes?"

Specific – "Bhaskar, when our guests get here, make sure you say 'Hi.' Then you can go to your room and play."

Vague – "When we get to the store, please be a nice girl."

Specific – "When we get to the store, remember that we aren't buying any candy. I'd like you to help me pick out the things on our list and put them in the cart. You can also push the shopping cart. Okay?"

Vague – "That was a nice story you wrote for English class, Sameer."

Specific – "Sameer, you did a nice job on that story for English class. You used complete sentences and all of the grammar was correct. The topic of prejudice was excellent! It was really controversial and interesting."

Vague – "Rahul, don't eat like a pig!"
Specific – "Rahul, you're making grunting noises while you eat. Please take smaller bites and don't make any noises."

These statements include specific descriptions of what each child said or did. When you specifically describe your children's behavior, it's more likely that they will receive clear messages.

Summary

One final thought about clear messages: The most important part of being specific when describing your children's misbehavior is that they understand that you dislike their behavior, not them. You are upset and displeased with the way your child is acting, but you always love your child. That's why you are taking the time to teach another way to behave.

Later in the book you will see how clear messages fit into a framework for praising and correcting your kids. Giving clear messages helps your children change their behavior and helps you become a much better teacher. Clear messages are crucial to making all the other teaching techniques work. In the next chapters, we'll add another valuable part of our teaching methods – giving consequences.

Notes

Chapter 3

Consequences

Consequences are at work all of the time. We face them every day – on our job, at home, with friends, and so on. If we don't get our work done, the boss criticizes us. If we don't remember to take the dog outside, he leaves a calling card on the floor. If we compliment a friend, he returns the pleasantry. Consequences affect all of us, positively and negatively.

Giving consequences to our kids is essential. Consequences teach kids to think. Consequences help children learn that their actions lead to results, both positive and negative. Children learn that life is full of choices and the choices they make greatly influence what happens to them. When parents give effective consequences, children learn successful ways to behave.

Consequences Change Behavior

Knowing how to effectively use consequences to teach our kids is very important. Because consequences have the power to change behavior, it makes sense that we should use them to benefit our kids. You've probably used consequences many times before – "grounding" your child for coming home late, letting your teen go out on a weekend night for helping around the house, and offering dessert only after the dinner is finished. These all are examples of consequences.

But, simply giving a consequence doesn't mean that kids are automatically going to change their behavior. Throughout this book, we emphasize a combination of clear messages and consequences when teaching your children. This combination, coupled with your love and affection, is very effective.

Let's look at some of the elements of effective consequences. Basically, there are two primary kinds of consequences – positive and negative.

> **Positive consequences** are things people like and are willing to work to get. Behavior that is followed by a positive consequence is more likely to occur again. Rewards and privileges are forms of positive consequences.

> **Negative consequences** are things people don't like and want to avoid. Basically, negative consequences encourage people to change their actions so that they won't receive more negative consequences. Behavior that is followed by a negative consequence is less likely to occur again (or will not occur as frequently). Removing a reward or privilege is a negative consequence.

Now, let's examine some qualities to consider when you choose a consequence.

> **Importance.** The consequence has to mean something to your child. One way to find out what is important to your child is to watch what he or she does during free time. For example, let's say your young son likes to watch cartoons, invite friends over, and ride his bicycle. These things mean something to him and are enjoyable activities. These everyday and special activities can be used as effective consequences. Taking away or giving something that isn't of interest to your child will not help change the behavior you want to change.

> **Immediacy.** This means that parents should give a consequence right after a behavior occurs. If you can't give the consequence right away, give it as soon as possible. Delaying a consequence reduces its impact and weakens the connection between the behavior and the conse-

quence. If you were to take away play time for something your five-year-old daughter did last week, she may be confused and think that you were tremendously unfair.

Frequency. This refers to the number of times a consequence is given. If you give the same consequence too often or too seldom, it loses its effectiveness. For example, if you were to give your son a fruitcake (assuming he loved fruitcake) each time he helped around the house, he might work like crazy to earn the fruitcake for awhile, but over time his helpfulness may decrease. Why? He would get tired of fruitcake and would not be as interested in working to earn it.

Size. Typically, parents should try to give the smallest consequence they think will be effective. This works for both positive and negative consequences. If you think that allowing your child to have a friend stay over Saturday night will be incentive enough for her to keep her room clean during the week, use that as the positive consequence. On the other hand, grounding your daughter for a month for not cleaning her room would be too big a negative consequence. A less severe consequence (for example, not allowing her to have her friend stay over) would probably get the job done.

Also, giving large positive consequences for minor behaviors may result in a "spoiled" child – one who gets too much for doing too little. On the other hand, giving large negative consequences for relatively small misbehaviors may result in a child who always feels punished. Always try to match the size of the consequence to the importance of the behavior.

Contingency. This is commonly called "Grandma's rule," because wise grandmothers used this long before it ever showed up in a book. Basically, it means that an activity (a privilege your child likes) is available after your child finishes a specified task. That is, one activity is contingent on the other. For example:

"You can watch TV **after** you have finished your homework."

"You can go outside **after** you make your bed and put your dirty clothes in the laundry basket."

"**After** you're finished with the dishes, you can call your friend."

These are all examples of Grandma's rule – giving a privilege after, not before, a specified task is completed. This contingency rule can be used with kids of all ages.

When Consequences Don't Work

Parents occasionally tell us that no matter what they try, the consequences they have used didn't work with their kids. It is possible that their children have problems too severe for them to handle. In that case, they need to see a professional counselor. More often than not, however, there are some basic reasons for ineffective consequences. The most frequent problems occur when parents aren't aware or don't use the five qualities just mentioned: Importance, immediacy, frequency, size, and contingency.

There also could be several other reasons why consequences don't work. We'll touch on a couple here.

First, parents sometimes give many negative consequences and neglect giving positive consequences. As a result, the negative consequences lose their effectiveness and the parents are viewed as punishing. The parents aren't providing a balance between positive and negative consequences. The kids, logically, go elsewhere to get positive consequences. It's just too darn unpleasant being around their parents.

The second reason is that parents don't always give consequences enough time to work. They often expect a consequence to change a behavior the first time it is used. This typically isn't the case. Change takes time. Your kids learned to behave the way they do over a long period of time. So don't give up if a change in behavior is not seen immediately. Be patient, look for small improvements, and give the consequences time to work.

A final reason is that some parents mistake privileges for rights. Of course, most kids will try to convince their parents that everything is a right. If parents treat privileges as rights, they limit what they can use for consequences. The rights of kids include the right to nourishment, communication with others, clothing, and so on. Watching TV, going out with friends, receiving allowance, using family possessions, and similar things, all are privileges that can and should be monitored by the parent and used by the child with the parent's approval. The list of rewards in the next chapter will help you identify privileges that can be used as consequences with your children.

Plan Ahead

Some parents have told us that when the time came to actually give a consequence, they had a hard time coming up with an effective one. Therefore, it's wise to set up both positive and negative consequences in advance. It is helpful to make a general list of consequences for situations or problems that occur frequently. This leads to choosing effective consequences.

One other thing. Your children should be aware of the consequences you have come up with. Don't hesitate to post established consequences, both positive and negative, on your refrigerator door or in your children's rooms. Consequences shouldn't be surprises. In fairness to your kids, they should be aware of what they will get for behaving well or what they will lose for misbehavior. In our chapter on charts and contracts, we talk about helping your child set and reach reasonable goals. Parents tell us that this also is a good way to spell out positive and negative consequences for their children.

Giving Consequences

The chapters in the following sections of the book outline steps for effectively giving consequences to your child. Until you finish those chapters, these few hints will help you be aware of how your behavior affects the outcome of a consequence. When delivering a consequence, remember to:

- Be clear. Make sure your child knows what the consequence is and what he or she did to earn it.
- Be consistent. Don't give a big consequence for a behavior one time and then ignore the same behavior the next time.
- Be brief. Don't lecture. This is especially true with younger children. Calmly let your children know what they did and what the consequence for it will be.
- Follow through. If you set up a plan for your child to earn a positive consequence, be sure he or she gets the reward after doing what is needed. Likewise, if you give a negative consequence, don't let your child talk you out of it. If you later feel that what you did was unreasonable or done out of anger, apologize and adjust the consequence accordingly.
- Let your behavior match the consequence. Be pleasant and enthusiastic when giving positive consequences. When giving negative consequences, be calm and matter-of-fact. At the very least, remain as calm as you can. Yelling and screaming are not effective when giving negative consequences. Kids can't hear your words, they can only hear your anger. Our experience with parents tells us that kids are more likely to respond better and learn more from parents who are calm and reasonable, especially when they are giving negative consequences to their children.

Warnings

Warnings mean you are merely threatening to give consequences, but never do – "If you don't stop that, I'll take your game away," or "You know you're not supposed to act that way. Next time, I'm going to ground you." Kids quickly figure out that you're not going to follow through with what you say. So, they begin ignoring your warnings. You and your consequences lose their effectiveness.

If you told your child that you would take the game away for a certain misbehavior, and the misbehavior occurs, then take the game away. This helps your child understand what behaviors are acceptable and unacceptable. It also helps your children make the connection between their behaviors and the consequences they receive. Otherwise, what you say not only is confusing but also creates a guessing game for your child: "Can I get away with it this time? Mom warned me three times so far and nothing's happened yet."

Please remember: Warnings don't work!

Summary

Appropriate consequences teach children successful ways to behave. They can help strengthen positive behaviors and weaken negative behaviors. There are five qualities that make consequences effective: importance, immediacy, frequency, size, and contingency. In the next two chapters, we will talk about the different types of positive and negative consequences you can use.

Notes

Chapter 4

Positive Consequences

In the last chapter, the two basic principles we covered were:

- Negative consequences are used to stop or decrease problem behavior.
- Positive consequences are used to increase or encourage desirable behavior.

In this chapter, we talk about positive consequences. Positive consequences can be a parent's best friend because they are used to increase positive behavior. Positive consequences also can be referred to as rewards. Generally, rewards are things that people like or enjoy. Therefore, when we use the term "reward," we mean any type of consequence that makes behavior occur again.

Using positive consequences is one way to increase the amount of time that kids spend doing positive things. If parents give only negative consequences, they run the risk of becoming a negative consequence themselves. In such situations, children may want to avoid their parents. On the other hand, when you give positive consequences, your kids find that spending time with you is more enjoyable. This gives you even more opportunities to use praise and positive consequences.

Parents who balance negative and positive consequences are viewed as more fair and reasonable by their children. Parents who consistently use positive consequences are more pleasant and effective and kids are more likely to listen to them.

Bribes

The idea of positive consequences (rewards) is viewed with skepticism by some parents. To them, it seems that kids are being bribed or paid off for doing what they're expected to do. However, rewards are a natural part of daily life. They can range anywhere from obvious things like merit raises at work to subtle things like a smile or a wink. These are given for acceptable behavior – behavior that we want to see again.

Bribery occurs when rewards are given in the presence of inappropriate behavior. Giving a child a candy bar when he's crying and screaming in the grocery store in order to shut him up is a bribe. (It may seem necessary for our sanity, but it's still a good example of a bribe.) The parent feels forced to do anything to stop the child's negative behavior – "Okay, you can have the candy, just shut up!" In essence, the child is rewarded for being a brat. If this scenario occurs frequently enough, the result is a child who always wants a reward before he'll act as the parent wants. Even though the candy was a reward and worked to silence the child, guess what happens the next time the parent is in the checkout lane? Right – crying and screaming, and demanding a candy bar. The child has been bribed and wants another bribe before acting appropriately.

Remember, don't give positive consequences to stop inappropriate behavior – those are bribes. Only give positive consequences for positive behavior.

Positive Consequences That Work

Something that is a reward for one person may not be a reward for someone else. This is sort of like the old saying "different strokes for different folks." The following list summarizes a variety of positive consequences that parents have used with their children. Using the examples as a guide, identify what your children like to do and write those preferences on a sheet of paper. Keep the list handy until you have a pretty good idea about which positive consequences work with your child.

Activities – What everyday activities does your child like to do? For example, video games, cricket, watching sitcoms, making snacks, and reading.

Possessions – What kinds of material articles does your child like? For example, sweatshirts, WWF cards, comic books, dolls, music cassettes or CDs.

Special activities – What special activities does your child like to do? For example, going to a cricket match, visiting the zoo, going to a movie, having a friend stay overnight.

Food – What are your child's favorite foods and beverages? For example, popcorn, Popsicles, pizza, cola, waffers, french fries, pav-bhaji, fruit juice. **Note: Do not use meals as a negative consequence; for example, taking away a balanced meal and making your child eat bread and water. Children have the right to proper nutrition.** In terms of consequences, "Food" refers to special snacks or types of food.

People – Who does your child like to spend time with? For example, you, friends, the child's grandparents or cousins, school teachers.

Attention – What specific kinds of verbal and physical attention from you and others does your child like? For example, hugs, smiles, time with you, compliments, high fives, pat on the back, and praise.

Other rewards – Is there anything else that your child likes, is interested in, or would like to spend time doing? Is there a favorite activity, or something that he or she has wanted to do but hasn't yet done?

Finally, all parents enjoy having a list of consequences that don't cost money. You can't buy something every time your child behaves well. Even if you could, it isn't necessarily healthy and you'll likely end up with a spoiled child. Remember, positive attention, praise, and encouragement are some of the most effective positive consequences a parent has – and they cost nothing!!!

The following list includes some additional examples of positive consequences that are "freebies":

Positive Consequences That Cost No Money

Stay up late
Messy room for a day
Stay out late
Leave radio on at night
Have a friend over
Sleep downstairs or outside
Go over to a friend's house
Pick the TV program
Extra TV time
Pick an outing
Play video game
One less chore
Shorter study period
Pick a movie
Decide where to go for dinner
Mom or Dad read a story at night
Stay up late reading
Play game with Mom or Dad
Use car
Sleep in late
Extra phone time
Plan the meal
Special snacks
Sit at the head of the table
Trip to the library, pet store, park, etc.
Extra night out with friends
Permission for a special event
Family Dinner
Extra time on the computer
Riding bicycle or going to zoo with parents
Indoor picnic
Make your own breakfast
Go window shopping

Pairing Consequences with Behavior

In Chapter 6, "Effective Praise," we present a method that combines your attention and approval with positive consequences. Remember to think about the qualities that make consequences effective (i.e. importance, immediacy, frequency, size, and contingency). The table below shows some possible pairings of positive consequences and children's behavior.

Behavior – Your 16-year-old daughter comes home on time for six weekends in a row.
Consequence – You can increase curfew by 30 minutes.

Behavior – Your 10-year-old son finishes his homework right after school.
Consequence – He gets to play outside for 30 minutes.

Behavior – Your four-year-old puts on his pajamas and gets into bed on time.
Consequence – You can read him a story tonight and give him a piggyback ride to bed tomorrow night.

Behavior – Your 7-year-old and 11-year-old play nicely together.
Consequence – You can fix them some popcorn while they watch a movie you've picked out.

Behavior – Your 13-year-old son helps his younger sister with her homework.
Consequence – You can play catch with him in the yard.

These examples will help prepare you for the chapter on Effective Praise. In that chapter, we cover how to use the clear message/consequence combination to further encourage your child's desirable behaviors.

Summary

The more you use positive consequences, the more likely you are to see positive behavior. Please remember that the most powerful rewards for children can be praise and positive attention from you. Keep up the good work. Continue to focus on the positive things your kids do – positive consequences work!

Notes

Chapter 5

Negative Consequences

"I hate you."
"I don't have to do anything I don't want to!"
"I was only an hour late. What's the big deal?"
"But, why do I have to clean my room? None of my friends clean theirs."

Kids are going to say and do things parents don't like. All kids are going to misbehave at some time. When they do, they should receive negative consequences. As you learned before, consequences help change behavior. If the consequences are given in a firm, fair, and consistent manner, they will be effective (and so will you).

This chapter will focus on using two forms of negative consequences – taking away a privilege for misbehavior and adding chores.

Taking Away a Privilege

When a problem behavior occurs, one type of negative consequence is the removal of a privilege. Some situations are tailor-made for this. For example, if your teenage daughter comes home an hour late, you may remove part of the privilege (having her come home an hour earlier next time she goes out), or if this is a frequent problem, she may lose the privilege of going out altogether. Similarly, if your two kids are arguing about which TV show to watch, you can shut off the TV until they settle their differences, or they could lose TV for the rest of the evening. Taking away privileges typically is an effective negative consequence for most children.

Give negative consequences in the same way you give positive consequences - in other words, pair the behavior with the consequence. For example, you could say to your teenager, "Sonia, because you're one hour late, you can't go out tomorrow night." To your two kids arguing over the TV, you could say, "Babu and Ratnesh, you're arguing about which show to watch. Please shut the TV off until you can calmly come to me with a solution."

Time-Out

For young children, losing privileges for short amounts of time can be very effective. One way for this to happen is by using what's called "Time-Out." Time-Out means time away from all those fun things in a child's life. It is a way of disciplining your young child without raising your hand or your voice. Basically, Time-Out involves having your child sit in one place for a certain amount of time. You can easily see that most kids wouldn't like Time-Out because they would rather be doing fun things.

Immediately following a problem behavior, describe that behavior to your child and send (or take) your child to Time-Out. Say this calmly and only once. Do not reason or explain or lecture. Arguing, threatening, raising your voice, or spanking should not be used. Avoid giving your child a lot of attention at this time.

Have a convenient place in mind for your Time-Out area. It doesn't have to be the same place each time. A kitchen chair, a couch, a footstool, or a step will all work. Make sure the area is safe, well-lit, and free from "fun distractions" like the TV or radio or toys.

Before you ever begin using Time-Out, explain to your child what Time-Out is, which problem behaviors it will be used for, and how long it will last. For example; you could say, "When I ask you to put your toys away and you start crying and throwing your toys, you will have to go sit on a chair in the kitchen for three minutes. I'll start the timer on the stove and when it buzzes you can get up." Then practice having your child go to the chair when you ask.

As a general rule, a child should spend one minute in Time-Out for every year of his or her age. In other words, if your child is three years old, quiet time should last no longer than three minutes. Your kids may think it's fun the first time you practice, but it's quite likely they won't be as pleased in an actual Time-Out situation. Therefore, it's very important that you do what you can to specifically explain the process beforehand.

During Time-Out, your child is to be quiet and sit calmly in the chair. Complaining and angry statements do not count toward "quiet time." On the other hand, fidgeting and talking in a soft voice probably should count. If your child cries or throws a tantrum, it doesn't count toward quiet time. If you start the time because your child is quiet but then starts to cry or tantrum again, wait until your child is quiet and start the time over again.

Your child must remain seated and be quiet to get out of Time-Out. If your child decides he's had enough and gets out of the chair, calmly return him to the chair. If this happens several times (and it often does when you first begin Time-Out), keep returning your child to the chair. If you get tired or other activities take you away from your Time-Out task, you can tell your child to leave the chair and use a different consequence. Your child may lose playing with the toy, friends may have to go home, or the TV may stay off for a certain amount of time. At a time when your child is calm, practice using Time-Out again. Practice it often enough that your child begins staying in the chair in actual Time-Out situations.

It's very likely that early in the process your child may cry, say some nasty things about you, throw things, or make a mess. Ignore anything that is not dangerous to your child, yourself, or your home. Most negative behavior is an attempt to get you to change your mind about this Time-Out thing.

When the Time-Out period is over, ask your child, "Are you ready to get up?" Your child must answer yes in some way that's agreeable to you – a nod or an "Okay" work just fine. Then you can say that Time-Out is over.

Adding Chores

Adding chores is an effective method for teaching responsibility. Chores take time and effort from your child, time that could be spent playing or doing something fun.

In some instances, the chore can relate directly to the problem. For example, your son can vacuum the carpet after he tracks dirt into the house.

Coming up with a related consequence isn't always easy. Nor is it necessary. Chores that are unrelated to the behavior can be just as effective at changing the behavior. For example, your son comes home late. After you ask him why he was late, he begins arguing and making excuses. After he calms down, you let him know that he can't go out the next night because he was late (related consequence – loss of privilege) and that he has to help clean the house for arguing with you (unrelated chore). Both consequences should be effective at reducing those behavior problems in the future.

The process of adding chores is simple. Your son is supposed to pick up his clothes instead of leaving them on the floor. If he doesn't, you can have him gather the dirty clothes from every family member and put them in the hamper. Adding this chore is a way to correct his behavior and teach responsibility.

Here are some examples of how chores can be used as consequences for kids.

- Your daughter breaks a friend's toy. To teach her responsibility, she must earn money to buy her friend a new toy by doing extra chores around the home.
- Your daughter borrows the car and returns it on time. However, the inside of the car is littered with numerous food and candy wrappers. She wants to call her best friend and talk to her. You decide that she is to clean out the car before she can make the call.
- Your sons are arguing about who gets to use the phone. Their consequence is to fold a load of laundry together until they can decide how to take turns on the phone.

- Your son and daughter are fighting about who last put away the clean dishes. So they can practice how to get along, they have to put away the dishes together for the next three days.

Here is a list of chores that you can use as consequences when you "add chores." Add chores in areas that are different from the routine chores kids normally do as part of their family responsibilities.

Folding laundry
Putting laundry away
Making your brother's or sister's bed
Cleaning one (or several) rooms
Arranging the bookshelf
Mowing the grass
Taking out the trash
Collecting the trash from throughout the house
Helping your brother (sister) with his chores
Dusting furniture
Cleaning the closet
Washing some or all of the windows in your home
Washing the dishes
Helping mom in making breakfast
Watering the plants
Taking care of dog
Helping your brother (sister) put toys away
Washing, drying, or putting away the dishes
Cleaning the dining table
Cleaning the bathroom
Cleaning the kitchen sink
Cleaning the bedroom
Shaking the rugs

It's up to you to decide how often a chore should be done, and to define exactly what the child should do. Take into account the age and ability of your children. Also, adjust the consequences to fit the severity of the problem behavior. Remember to use the smallest consequence necessary to change the behavior.

One variation that parents tell us works well is the "chore jar." Parents write various chores on small pieces of paper and put them in the jar. When their child misbehaves, the parents may opt to have their child select a chore from the chore jar. This makes it easier for parents because the consequences are made up ahead of time and are readily available. It works best if parents tell their kids ahead of time about the chore jar and how it will work. Many parents use the chore jar for their child's common misbehaviors like talking back or not following directions right away.

Some parents have their kids put the slips of paper in a second jar after a chore has been completed. Then, when the first jar is empty, another chore jar is ready to use.

Are You Giving a Negative Consequence?

Sometimes, parents make the mistake of assuming that a consequence is negative when it isn't. We encourage you to look at the effect a consequence has on the behavior you want to change. If the behavior stops or decreases in frequency, you've given a negative consequence. If the behavior continues or occurs more often, you've given a positive consequence.

For example, one mother told us that her six-year-old continually fidgeted and talked in temple. She told him that he couldn't come with her next time if he continued causing problems in temple. Sure enough, that kid fidgeted like crazy and talked more than ever. He didn't want to be in temple to begin with! His mother's "negative consequence" actually encouraged more problem behaviors. The behavior she wanted to stop (fidgeting) actually increased. She had given him a positive consequence.

We suggested that she do one of the following:

Remove a privilege – if he fidgets and talks loudly in temple, he can't play with his friend visiting temple.
Add a chore – if he fidgets or talks in temple, he has to help Mom clean the kitchen.

Actually, the mother used both methods. And they worked. After a few minor prompts, the young boy learned to sit quietly in temple.

Pay close attention to the effect a consequence has on the behavior you want to change. If the problem behavior has decreased or ended altogether, you gave an effective negative consequence.

The Snowball Effect

One problem with negative consequences is that parents can lose sight of when to stop giving them. If one consequence doesn't work, parents often try another that is harsher. They begin piling negative consequences on top of negative consequences. This can lead to an upward spiral where the parent ends up grounding the child for the next five years, or something outlandish like that. This often happens when parents are frustrated and upset. Children know what "buttons" to push, and parents can quickly lose their patience. That's when "the snowball effect" usually takes place.

For example, Anita's dad asked her to clean her room. She didn't do the chore so her dad took away her telephone privileges for a weekend. Her room was messy the next day. For this, she lost a week of TV privileges. The room didn't get any cleaner and her father got madder and more frustrated. So he added another month without phone privileges, another week without TV, and told her that she couldn't come out of her room until it was spotless.

Whew! This wasn't just the snowball effect; this became an avalanche! In three days, this girl lost just about all communication with the outside world! This was a good example of how a parent can get carried away with giving ineffective negative consequences. Instead of repeating negative consequences in rapid-fire succession, step back and look at the effects of the consequence on the behavior. Change the consequence if necessary, but don't let it snowball out of control. More is not necessarily better. Since the consequences given by this father were unreasonable (and impossible to carry out), we suggested that he go back, talk to Anita, and set up the following plan:

1. He helps Anita clean her room.
2. In return, Anita helps him clean the drawing room.

If both parts of the plan are completed, Anita gets her privileges back. To help Anita keep the room clean consistently, we helped the father find a way to put Grandma's Rule into practice – each day that Anita cleans her room, she gets to use the phone and watch her favorite TV show. This practical solution worked. Anita's room was not spotless, but it was clean much more often than it was dirty. And, Dad knew exactly what consequence he would use whether the room was clean or dirty. Dad learned how to avoid the snowball effect and still give a negative consequence that worked.

How to Give Negative Consequences

The effectiveness of your consequences depends, in part, on how you give them. An angry response is not going to work; it usually results in more problems. Our experience tells us that kids respond better and learn more from adults who are pleasant and positive, even when they are giving negative consequences. Although staying calm is crucial to effective teaching, parents tell us it's one of the hardest things for them to do. For that reason, we wrote a chapter that gives suggestions which may help you keep your cool during stressful times with your kids. See Chapter 9, "Staying Calm."

Parents can easily get upset when they give negative consequences. Not many of us like to deal with problem behavior. Therefore, you have to be aware of how you give negative consequences. Part of remaining calm means being in control of your own behavior. Don't use a harsh voice tone, talk fast, point fingers, call names, and so on. In other words, don't become more of a negative consequence than the consequence itself. After you give a negative consequence, think about what it was and how you gave it.

More information on giving negative consequences can be found in Chapter 10, "Corrective Teaching," and Chapter 11, "Teaching Self-Control." Parents have found that both of these methods provide them with frameworks for dealing with negative behavior.

Summary

Finding effective negative consequences is a challenge for parents, but it is not impossible. If your children misbehave, stay calm and do one of the following – remove all or part of a privilege, or add work. Be logical, fair, and consistent and you'll be on the road to using effective consequences.

Notes

Chapter 6

Effective Praise

Praise is powerful. Praising your child is one of the most important things you can do as a parent.

Praise is nourishment. It helps your child grow emotionally, just as food helps your child grow physically.

Focus on the Positive

Praise is not a new concept; we're all familiar with it. But many of us don't use it as often as we should. Why? One of the reasons is that we have been trained to see negatives. It is easy to see what people do wrong. Some companies have a philosophy they call the "3:11" rule. For example, if you go to a restaurant and have a good meal, you'll probably tell three other people about it. On the other hand, if you get a lousy meal, you'll probably tell 11 other people! Think about it; isn't that focusing on the negative?

Parents often focus on the negative, too. It's easy for them to see the mistakes and shortcomings of their children. In fact, one parent we worked with told us, "When I was growing up, the only time I knew I was doing something right was when I didn't hear anything from my parents. But I always heard from them when I did something wrong!"

Focusing on the negative is easy. And it takes some effort to refocus so we see the good things our kids do. We have found one thing to be true time and time again – praise works wonders. If you consistently use praise, you will notice dramatic improvements over time. When you zero in on as many positive things as you can, your kids will feel better about themselves. The positive attention that comes along with praise also makes them feel cared for and loved.

When to Use Praise

It helps to focus on the following general areas when looking for opportunities to praise your kids.

1. Things your kids already do well (and maybe you take for granted)
2. Improvements
3. Positive attempts at new skills

For example, your kids may already get up on time, or clean their rooms, or turn off their lights. Praise them for the things they already do well if you haven't mentioned your appreciation recently. Most likely, they will continue to do these things since you took the time to notice.

Make sure you recognize when your kids are making improvements, no matter how small. No one learns how to do something well right away. When your child was learning to walk, you probably praised each and every improvement – from first standing alone, to taking that first awkward step, to finally putting a series of steps together. You praised improvements.

Likewise, when your kids are learning new skills, they may be more likely to stick with the process if you praise them for their positive attempts at learning the new skill. Your enthusiasm and attention to your children's attempts at success can carry over to many areas of their lives, regardless of age – accepting criticism without arguing, admitting mistakes, offering to help, talking with guests, making friends, and so on. Seize every opportunity to recognize positive attempts to learn new skills. Praise the fact that your kids are trying.

How to Use Effective Praise

The easiest way to praise someone is to say things like, "Fantastic," "Great," or "Keep up the good work." This is what we call general praise. It's a quick and easy way to focus on the positive things your kids do. These words show your affection and approval and really encourage your kids to do well. It takes so little time and effort but the benefits are so great!

But you can make general praise even better. By adding a couple of steps, you can increase the number of good things your kids do. That's why we make a distinction between general praise and what we call "Effective Praise."

The Steps of Effective Praise

Consistently using Effective Praise will result in more positive behaviors from your children. Consistently "catching 'em being good" results in kids who like themselves and grow in self-confidence.

Let's look at the steps of Effective Praise and examine the importance of each step.

- ***Show your approval***
- ***Describe the positive***
- ***Give a reason***

Show Your Approval

Kids like to hear nice things said about them (who doesn't?) and they'll work hard to get more praise in the future. When you combine a sign of your approval with specific praise, your praise is that much more meaningful.

There are numerous words that show your satisfaction with your child's behavior. And, for goodness sakes, show a little excitement!

Awesome!... Terrific!... Wow!... You're right on target!... I love you... I'm impressed!... Super!... Amazing!... That's great!... Wonderful!... Magnificent!... Excellent!... (Doesn't it make you feel better just saying these words?)

There also are numerous actions that convey your approval: Hugging them... Kissing them... Picking them up... Winking or smiling at them... Giving them a "thumbs up" or an A-Okay sign... Ruffling their hair... Giving them "five"... Nodding your head... Clapping for them....

Showing your approval lets kids know that you're excited about what they're doing. In turn, they will be more satisfied with themselves.

Describe the Positive

After you have given a praise statement, describe the specific behaviors you liked. Make sure your kids understand what they did so that they can repeat the behavior in the future. Give them clear messages. Praise what you just saw or heard your child do well. For example, "Sushila, thanks for cleaning the dishes and helping me put the leftovers away." Or, "Subash, I'm glad you washed your hands after you went to the bathroom."

Remember to use words your kids understand. Make it brief and to the point. Just let your child know what was done well.

Give a Reason

Children benefit from knowing why a behavior is helpful to them or others. It helps them understand the relationship between their behavior and what happens to them.

For example, if your teenager volunteers to clean up the dinning room before guests come over (and then does it), explain why that behavior is helpful. For example, "Cleaning the dinning room really saved us a lot of time. We have time to get everything finished before guests come over."

You could give your teen lots of other reasons why helping out is important: "Helping others is a real plus. If you do that on the job, your boss is more likely to give you a raise."

Or you could say, "Since you helped out, I'll have time to take you over to your friend's house when you want to go. I don't know if I would have had time if you hadn't helped."

Giving your child a reason links the relationship between his or her behavior and the consequences or outcomes. Reasons are particularly valuable when they can demonstrate the benefits your child may receive, either immediately or in the future. The reasons should be brief, believable, age-appropriate, and kid-related.

Here are some descriptions of kids' behaviors and corresponding kid-related reasons that other parents have given:

- It's important to accept criticism from your teacher so that he knows that you're taking responsibility for the mistakes on your homework. He'll be more likely to help you with the problems in the future.
- When you're home on time, I will trust you more and probably will let you go out more often.
- Putting your clean clothes away will mean you'll be able to find them the next time you want to wear them.
- When you spend more of your time reading, you're likely to learn more and do better in school than when you sit and watch TV all evening.
- Driving the car without talking on your mobile means you'll be able to hear important sounds – like a siren from a police car or ambulance.
- Picking up your things is important because people won't step on them and break them.
- If you do your homework right after school, you'll have more time to play outside when I get home.
- Sharing your toys with others is helpful because they're more likely to share their toys with you.

Optional Reward

Occasionally, you may want to add a fourth step to Effective Praise – a reward. When you are especially pleased with a certain behavior, or your child has made a big improvement in a certain area, you can reward your child with a special privilege.

Rewards can be large or small, that's up to you. Just as long as the size of the reward fits the behavior you want to encourage.

Examples of Effective Praise

Let's look at a brief example of Effective Praise: Your teenage son just called to tell you where he was.

Show your approval
"Thanks for calling me."

Describe the positive
"I'm really glad that you let me know where you were and why you'll be a little late."

Give a reason
"Calling me shows a lot of sensitivity and shows that I can trust you."

In this brief scenario, your child learned specifically what he did right and why it was so important. You increased the likelihood that he will call the next time he's out.

Let's take a look at some more examples of Effective Praise:

Show your approval
"Mahesh, that's great!"

Describe the positive
"You tied your tennis shoes all by yourself!"

Give a reason
"Now, you won't have to wait for me to do it for you."

Show your approval
"Way to go, Ramesh!"

Describe the positive
"You did your homework before watching TV."

Give a reason
"Now, you won't have to do it late at night."

Optional reward
"Would you like some popcorn while you watch the movie?"

Show your approval
"Kris, wnat a nice job!"

Describe the positive
Our neighbor told me that you coached their son so well while you helped him do his homework.

Give a reason
Since you coached their son so nicely by helping him to understand the subject, they now want you to also coach their other son.

Does Praise Always Work?

Some parents tell us that they praise their children, but it just doesn't seem to make any difference in their kids' behavior. Usually, we find that these parents only praise outstanding achievements or momentous occasions. They are missing many opportunities to focus on the positive. We ask them to look for little things to praise, also. After parents begin looking closely for small improvements, they notice many positive changes in their kids' behavior. In addition, the parents feel they get along better with their kids. This is not coincidence. Praise works.

Other parents have asked us, "Why should I praise my kids for something that they're supposed to do?" Good question. We answer them with another question. "Do you like being recognized for the things you do well, regardless of whether you're supposed to do them? Do you like to hear your boss tell you what a good job you're doing?" Most parents say "Of course." And then add, "And, I wouldn't mind hearing it a little more often." Enough said. We all like to hear about things we do well.

Additionally, we have had parents tell us that they praise their children often yet it doesn't seem to mean much. These parents tend to praise their kids for everything! Their praise is not contingent on their kids' positive behavior. It's no different than giving kids ice cream every time they turn around. Sooner or later, no matter how much a child likes ice cream, it's going to lose its attractiveness. Praise also loses its impact if it is dished up noncontingently.

Effective Praise, on the other hand, is both frequent and contingent. That's why it works! Parents provide praise and encouragement for very specific things their kids have done. This attention to specific behavior increases the likelihood that these same behaviors will occur again.

Summary

Each of your children gives you something to be happy about. Every kid does something that deserves praise. Make sure you recognize it, and most of all, tell them.

One final note. In interviews with some of the thousands of parents who have completed our parenting classes, they have consistently told us that Effective Praise has had a lasting impact on their families. Parents find themselves being more positive about their kids, and kids, in turn, are more positive about their parents. With Effective Praise, everyone wins.

Notes

Chapter 7

Preventive Teaching

Ben Franklin once said, "An ounce of prevention is worth a pound of cure." Old Ben was right; society's reliance on preventive measures is proof of that. We have fire drills; we have our cars tuned up; we go to the doctor for a physical exam. We do all of these precautionary things to prevent problems. While practicing a fire drill may not keep a fire from starting, it could prevent a catastrophe such as the loss of life in a fire. Prevention is both necessary and important.

An Ounce of Prevention

We've taken Ben's wisdom and applied it to parenting. We call our method Preventive Teaching. Preventive Teaching is our "ounce of prevention." We, as parents, should spend time teaching important skills to our kids before they need to use them. We can help our kids prevent problems from occurring. It stands to reason that when children know what is expected of them, and have the opportunity to prepare, they will be more successful.

You've probably used Preventive Teaching already – teaching your child how to safely cross the street, what number to dial in case of emergency, what clothes to wear when it's cold, and so on. You tried to anticipate and prevent problems your children might face and increase their chances for success. Preventive Teaching is teaching your child what he or she will need to know for a future situation and practicing it in advance.

When to Use Preventive Teaching

There are two types of situations in which you can use Preventive Teaching:

1. When your child is learning something new.
2. When your child has had difficulty in a past situation.

In each case, use Preventive Teaching **before** your child faces the new situation or **before** your child faces situations in which there was a problem. For example, if this is the first time your son is going to ask his teacher for an extra credit assignment, you may use Preventive Teaching to demonstrate how he might ask and how the teacher might respond. Or, if your daughter frequently argues when you ask her to hang up the phone, you can use Preventive Teaching before she makes a call so she can practice how to respond appropriately to your request. In both these examples, Preventive Teaching occurred before the child faced the actual situation. It's best to use Preventive Teaching when your child is calm and attentive, not after a misbehavior or when he or she is upset.

Of course, the Preventive Teaching areas you focus on will vary with each child, but all kids can learn something new or improve behaviors that have caused problems in the past. You may want your young son to learn how to make his own breakfast or how to make his bed. Or you may want your young daughter to improve in areas where she has had difficulties before, like playing nicely with others or getting to bed on time. For a young teen, you may want to teach how to invite someone (or to refuse) a party invitation or how to ride a scooter or motorcycle. Or, you may want him to improve in situations where he loses his temper or doesn't know how to respond to a teacher.

Preventive Teaching is a simple concept, but parents usually don't use it as often or in as many situations as they could. Here are some examples of situations in which other parents have used Preventive Teaching. Before their children faced a certain situation, they taught their children how to:

- Come in from playing when called (a prior problem).
- Ask for make-up work in school (something new).

- Apologize for getting in a fight (something new).
- Say "No" if someone offers alcohol (a prior problem).
- Make a presentation to classmates (something new).
- Sit quietly and not ask for candy in the store (a prior problem).
- Accept a "No" answer (a prior problem).
- Answer a police officer's questions (something new).

Chapter 16, "Social Skills," outlines other basic skills that you can teach your children. All of these can be taught using Preventive Teaching.

The Steps of Preventive Teaching

The steps of Preventive Teaching combine clear messages and kid-related reasons with a new step – practice. Practice gives your child an opportunity to see how they would use the skill before they get in the actual situation.

Let's look at the steps of Preventive Teaching:

- ***Describe what you would like***
- ***Give a reason***
- ***Practice***

Let's look at an example of Preventive Teaching. Your son is about to go outside to play and, on prior occasions, has had difficulty coming in when he's called. Before he goes outside, you:

Describe what you would like

"Rahul, when I call you to come in for dinner, let me know that you heard me by saying 'Okay' and then come in right away."

Give a reason

"If you come in right away, you'll have a better chance of having time to play after dinner."

Practice

"Let's pretend I've just called you in. What are you going to say and do? (Rahul says 'Okay' and that he will come inside) ...Great! Now run and have fun. Remember to come home right away when I call."

Let's look at the steps and see why each is important.

Describe what you would like

Before your children can do what you want, they must first know what it is that you expect. Be specific when you describe your expectations. Make sure your children understand. For example, your daughter argued with the referee at her last basketball game. Before her next game, you would teach her how to respond when she doesn't agree with the call. You might say, "Smita, tonight at the basketball game, you need to remain calm if the referee makes a call against you or your team. Try to keep your mouth closed, take a deep breath, and walk toward your coach when you get upset."

Give a Reason

Children, like adults, benefit from knowing why they should act a certain way. Reasons explain to a child how new skills and appropriate behaviors are helpful and important. They also teach how inappropriate behaviors are harmful. The best reasons, of course, are those that relate directly to the person's life. Simply saying to your kids, "Do it because I said so," is a command, not a reason. It does not give your kids any relationship between their actions and future benefits to them.

Sometimes it is difficult to come up with reasons that mean a lot to your kids at that time. Even if they don't immediately agree with what you are saying, at least they will know why you think it is important. That means a great deal since reasons indicate fairness and logic. Kids are much more likely to comply with what you say when you give reasons. If reasons are personal to the youth, they are more likely to accept what you are teaching. For example, "When you yell or get upset with the referee, it takes your mind off of the game and you don't play as well." Or, "When you stay calm after the ref makes a call, you'll get to stay in the game longer."

Practice

Knowing what to do and knowing how to do it are two different things. Any new skill needs to be practiced. You can tell your son how to ride a bicycle, but that hardly will ensure that he could hop right on and take off. Likewise, you can tell your daughter how to get away from the class bully, but she'll be more likely to be successful the next time the bully tries to get her lunch if she's had a chance to practice what she should do and say in that situation. It takes practice to become good at almost anything. Practice also increases the chances that your child will be successful.

Children occasionally are reluctant to practice – especially when being taught a new skill. They may feel embarrassed, or lack the self-confidence, or think that practicing is a waste of time. The fact of the matter is that practice actually eases embarrassment and raises kids' self-confidence in their abilities when they are faced with the real situation. Encourage them as they practice and use a lot of praise for trying.

When practicing with younger children, make practice fun, yet realistic. Parents report that their young children, in particular, enjoy practicing in many situations. The young children like to pretend and play different roles in the practices. This is a time for you to have fun with them and teach them some skills at the same time.

Older children and adolescents can be more of a challenge when it comes to practicing. With older kids, set up the practice step with words like, "Show me how you would handle..." or "Okay, in the same type of situation, what would you say to..." This gives older children an opportunity to demonstrate their ability without feeling like you are talking down to them.

After finishing the practice, praise areas that your child did well in and encourage your child to improve in areas that need improvement. Don't expect perfection the first time you practice. You can practice again if you need to. Or, you can practice later in the day.

If you are practicing a complex skill or a difficult situation, such as how to say "No" to peer pressure or using drugs, never promise that the actual situation will work out perfectly. Emphasize to your child that he or she is practicing possible ways to handle a situation and the outcome won't always be the same as the one you practice. You cannot ensure your children's success in every situation; you can only improve the odds.

Also, the more types of situations you can practice with your children, the more likely they are to succeed in the actual situations. You will be helping them learn more and more ways to solve problems.

In the previous example, you were teaching your daughter how to stay calm after a referee's call. When it's time for practice, you might say, "Okay, Smita, here's the situation. I'm the referee and I've just called a foul on you. Show me what you'll do to stay calm. Okay?"

Preventive Prompts

After using Preventive Teaching several times to teach a skill, you may only need to provide a reminder - a preventive prompt. For example, let's say that you have practiced with your daughter on how to stay calm when she gets upset with her friends. Before she goes out to play, you could say, "Remember, Smita, stay calm just like we practiced for your basketball games. Don't say anything and take a few deep breaths. Then walk away from them if you have to." The purpose of a preventive prompt is to get your child focused on what you have practiced.

Examples of Preventive Teaching

Let's look at some more examples of Preventive Teaching:

A teenage girl is going to a party with some friends and her mother wants to help her to be prepared to say "No" if anyone offers her an alcoholic beverage.

Describe what you would like

Mom – "We've talked about this before, Leela, but it's real important so I just want to go over it again before you go out tonight. Do you remember what you can say if someone offers you something to drink?"

Leela – "Yeah, mom. I should say, 'I won't drink because my parents would ground me. I wouldn't get to go out next week.'"
Mom – "Great! And if they kept pestering you?"
Leela – "I could say, 'I like you guys but if you keep bugging me about drinking, I'm just going to leave - I'm not going to drink, okay?'"

Give a reason

Mom – "Leela, I know that sometimes it's tough, but letting your friends know that you won't drink will help you stay out of trouble. Not only is drinking illegal, it's also dangerous. So as long as you stay away from drinking and drugs, I'll be more likely to let you go out with friends, okay?"

Practice

(In this situation Leela has already practiced saying what she would say to her friends so another practice here would not be necessary.)

A four-year-old boy argues frequently with his mom whenever she tells him that he can't do something. She knows he will want to play outside today so she uses Preventive Teaching before he asks.

Describe what you would like

Mom - "Mahesh, sometimes when I tell you 'No,' you argue and have a tantrum. Instead of fighting with me when you're upset, I want you to play a game with me. I want you to pretend like you're blowing out candles and breathe like this." (Mom then shows him how to take deep breaths and pretend like he's blowing out candles.)

Give a reason

Mom – "By blowing out the pretend candles, you'll be letting me know that you're upset but you won't get into trouble like you do when you have a tantrum. Then when you're finished blowing out all the candles, we can talk about why you're upset, okay?"

Practice

Mom – "Now, pretend that you're upset because I told you that you can't have a cookie. Show me how you'd blow out the candles to let me know that you're upset."

(Mahesh takes a deep breath and pretends to blow out the candles three times.)

Mom – "That's great! Blow out those candles whenever you feel like you're getting upset. Then we can talk about why you're upset."

A 16-year-old boy is going to the movie with a girl for the first time. His dad wants to teach him how to be a gentleman and hold the door open for the girl.

Describe what you would like

Dad – "Okay, Subhash, there are a few things that I want to talk to you about before you go to the movies with Mallika. First, you've gotta get to her house on time and that means taking the 5:20 bus. Next, I want you to introduce yourself to her mom. After saying namaste, then say something like, 'Hi, I'm Subhash. It's nice to meet you Mrs. Jogeshwari.' Finally, I want you to be sure to hold the door open for Mallika and let her go first through the door. Okay?"

Subhash – "Yeah, dad. I'll be fine. I don't know why you're making such a big deal about this."

Give a reason

Dad – "Well, if you make a good impression on her mom, she might let you go to the show with Mallika again. And if you treat Mallika with respect, she might actually agree to go to another movie with you."

Practice

Dad – "Now, let's say that I'm Mrs. Jogeshwari. Show me how you'd introduce yourself when she comes to the door. And remember to look at me and shake my hand." (Subhash shakes his dad's hand and introduces himself.) Dad - "Okay, now pretend I'm Mallika and show me how you'd hold the door open for me." (Eddie gets the door for his dad.)

Dad – "Very good, Subhash. I'm sure Mallika's mom will be impressed. Have a great time."

Summary

Preventive Teaching is a valuable tool for both parents and children. You can promote gradual behavior changes in areas where your children may be having problems and help them prepare for unfamiliar situations. Preventive Teaching can increase your children's self-confidence by showing them that they can learn how to change their behaviors and be successful. And, perhaps most importantly, Preventive Teaching allows you and your child to work toward goals together. Taking the time to be with your children and showing them that you care helps improve relationships, and that benefits the whole family.

It will be helpful to make two lists: one for the areas where your child can learn something new, and one for the areas where your child has had problems before. Then use Preventive Teaching in these situations over the next week. After using Preventive Teaching, look carefully for any improvements and praise your kids when they do improve.

Notes

Chapter 8

Clear Expectations

When we ask parents why they are taking our Common Sense Parenting classes, they frequently answer that they want less conflict with their children. Usually, this means they want their children to stop doing something negative. Or they want their children to start doing something positive. For example, they say that they don't want their child to throw a fit when they tell him to clean his room. Instead, they do want their child to say "Okay" and clean the room right away. Or they don't want their daughter to argue when she's told that she can't go to her friend's house. Instead, they do want her to calmly accept their "No" answers. These "Do's" and "Don'ts" are all examples of parents' expectations for their children's behavior. This chapter talks about these expectations: how to develop them, how to clarify them, and how to encourage improvements toward them.

Developing Clear Expectations

The first step in developing clear expectations is to identify those that are already in place in your family. The list below may help you focus on areas that other parents have used to organize and specify their expectations. On a separate sheet of paper, list some of the expectations you have for your kids.

Social – How to get along with others, greeting and conversation skills, how to interact with the opposite sex, offering to help others.

Academic – Study habits, school attendance and behavior, completing homework, respecting teachers and administrators, following school rules.

Family chores – Cleaning the bedroom, helping at mealtime, volunteering, picking up after yourself, helping with outside chores, helping clean the house.

Personal appearance and hygiene – Regular showers or baths, clean clothes, putting away personal items, using soap and deodorant, appropriate attire, jewelry.

Religious – Church attendance, prayer, volunteering for activities, living up to the family's religious standards.

Now that you have some examples of your own to work with, let's take a look at whether your expectations are reasonable for your children. To find out if they're reasonable, ask yourself, "Are these expectations appropriate for my kids' ages, abilities, and resources?"

Kids develop at their own unique pace and in their own unique ways. We won't go into a long description about developmental milestones for children. There are many good books that explain child development. But from a practical standpoint, there are limits to what we can expect from kids of all ages. For example, it would be reasonable to expect that an average six-year-old can learn how to set the dinner table. It would require teaching and assistance from you, but it is a reasonable expectation. However, it would be unreasonable to think that the same six-year-old could prepare the meal. Even with your best teaching, it is highly unlikely that a six-year-old could follow a recipe, measure ingredients accurately, and safely cook the meal on the stove. Expecting a six-year-old to prepare a meal would definitely be an unreasonable expectation. This expectation would be inappropriate for someone of his **age, abilities, and resources.**

How do you tell whether an expectation is reasonable or not? If you can answer "Yes" to all three of the following questions, then you probably have a reasonable expectation for your child.

◆ Have you **taught** the expectation to your children?

The chapters in this book describe how to teach your children the various skills they will need to be successful. In particular, you can use Preventive Teaching to teach your children what you expect of them. It is unreasonable to expect something from your kids if you haven't taught it to them.

◆ Can your children **understand** the expectation?

One way to check for understanding is to have your children describe in their own words what you've said to them. For example, it is likely that your six-year-old can repeat back to you a description of how and where to set plates and silverware. Your child may not use the exact words that you use, but the description will indicate whether your expectations were clear.

◆ Can your children **demonstrate** what you expect?

Ask your children to show you what you have taught. If they can demonstrate the task reasonably well, then your expectation is probably within your children's abilities.

The lists that follow are examples of parents' expectations for their children. For many families, these expectations are unwritten. For other families, parents and children have discussed the expectations and have them written down. However you choose to convey your expectations with your children, it helps to make sure that all family members are aware of them. You can discuss them individually by using Preventive Teaching or you can discuss them as a group at Family Meetings.

Expectations for Older Children

Please remember these are general examples. Your expectations will likely vary from these.

1. When you complete your homework and have it checked, you may watch TV or use the phone.
2. When you study or read at least one hour on Sunday through Thursday nights, you get to go out on Friday or Saturday night.
3. When you want to go out on the weekends, ask at

least two days in advance (Wednesday for Friday, Thursday for Saturday). This helps us avoid problems with using the car and helps organize a schedule.

4. In order to use the car, ask at least one day in advance. Bring it back with the same amount of gas, and be willing to wash it when we think it is necessary.
5. Please limit your phone calls to four 15-minute calls a night. All calls end before 10 o'clock.
6. Before asking to go anywhere or to do anything, complete all housework (make bed, clean room, put clothes where they belong) and school work.
7. If you disagree with an answer, disagree calmly without arguing. Then we will listen to you. When you argue, you will lose 15 minutes or more of your curfew.
8. Put your dirty clothes in the laundry pile. If you leave dirty clothes in your room, it will be your responsibility to fold the next load of wash.
9. Attend temple once a week with the family. Have at least one volunteer activity in the temple each month. If you don't feel well enough to go to temple you're probably not well enough to go out with your friends.
10. Before going out, be prepared to answer questions like: Where are you going? What are you going to do? Who will you be with? When do you plan to be back?

Expectations for Younger Children

1. Keep your feet off the furniture so you don't lose any of your play time.
2. When you come home, hang your coat where it belongs and put your shoes in your closet. Then, you may have a snack.
3. Everyone cleans their plate and puts it in the sink before having dessert.
4. Volunteer to either help set the table or help clean up after dinner.

5. Bedtime is at 10:00 and we start getting ready at 9:30. If you are ready for bed by 9:40, we'll have time to read a story.
6. Say your prayers before each meal and before going to bed.
7. Ask permission before you turn on the TV.
8. Flush the toilet and wash your hands after you go to the bathroom.
9. Wash your hands before meals.
10. Get your books and school supplies ready before you go to bed each night.

Clarifying Expectations

There are two important parts of clarifying expectations for your kids. The first part involves what you say and the second involves what you do.

What you say. Expectations are usually clearer and more effective when you describe them in a positive way, instead of telling your kids what not to do. There still will be times, however, when you use "don't" statements. Try to catch yourself and tag on a "do" description to help clarify the expectations for your child. For example, you might tell your four-year-old, "Don't draw on the wall." Then add, "When you want to draw, ask me for some paper and sit at the table to draw." By positively describing your expectations, you make it clear what your child should do in the future. Several other examples of **Don't and Do** expectations are listed below.

Don't – "When I ask you to help clean the house, don't talk back and roll your eyes."

Do – "When I ask you to help clean the house, say 'Okay' and start the job right away."

Don't – "I don't want you grabbing things from your sister."

Do – "Ask your sister to share when she has something that you want."

Don't – "Don't yell and complain when I tell you that you can't do something."

Do – "When you ask me to do something and I tell you 'No,' just say you understand. If you don't understand, calmly ask me to explain it to you."

Don't – "Don't sneak off and watch TV when you're supposed to be doing your homework."

Do – "Start your homework right away when you get home from school."

What you do. Making sure your children understand your expectations involves praising behavior that is consistent with your expectations and correcting behavior that does not match your expectations. If your kids do what's expected of them, let them know! If you expect them to do their homework right after school and you find them doing it, then use Effective Praise to encourage those behaviors. If you tell your kids "No" after they've asked to go to a friend's house, and they accept your answer by saying "Okay," then praise them for accepting your answer.

Likewise, if your children argue with you after you tell them "No," use Corrective Teaching to correct the problem. Letting them argue and whine after you tell them "No" on some occasions and correcting them on others is confusing. Clarity comes both from what you say and what you do in response to their behavior.

Also remember, your behavior should be consistent with your expectations for your children. (See page 80, "Consistency and Routines.") If you want your kids to disagree calmly, then give them a good example to follow when you have a disagreement with them. If you expect your children to attend religious services, then attend with them. If you want your kids to read more and do better in school, then turn the TV off and read with them. Many times, actions really do speak louder than words. So be a consistent and positive role model. Your children will have a much clearer understanding of your expectations when you do.

One final word about clear expectations. All parents need to have consistent expectations and methods of discipline. For some two-parent families or for joint families where several families live together, agreeing on expectations is a problem. One parent or adult family member may think the other is unreasonable, either too strict or too lax. It takes constant effort for two parents or the other family members who may have different approaches to parenting to set expectations they can all agree on. Parents, grandparents and/or aunts and uncles must learn to negotiate with one another. It also is important for them to agree not to argue about expectations in front of the children. When parents and adult family members can't agree, it makes life confusing and problematic for everyone in the family. It's worth the effort for parents and the other adult family members in the family to be consistent with their expectations for the children's behavior. In the long run, setting clear expectations benefits everyone in the family. Every adult in the family unit must set the example of how a multi-family is able to live in harmony together, so children pick up the concept of 'living in harmony' at a very early age.

Summary

Clear expectations help children understand what they should and shouldn't do. They provide a framework for positive behavior. Even though kids won't meet your expectations all of the time, consistency and patience will pay off in the long run. Remember to ask yourself three important questions: "Have I taught what I expect? Can my children understand what I expect? Can my children demonstrate what I expect?" If you answered 'Yes' to all of these questions, you're doing a great job of setting clear and reasonable expectations.

Consistency and Routines

Throughout this book, we talk about how important it is for parents to be consistent. By consistent we mean helping the kids know what is expected of them, and what they can expect from their parents, family, and community.

We're not recommending a rigid list of times and activities. But we are encouraging you to have daily routines for some activities. For example, one single mother and her two kids do most of their laundry on Sunday, and then spend the evening folding the laundry and watching TV together. Another parent with small children started getting her children ready for bed at 8:00 each evening. First, the TV got shut off, then the kids would get into their pajamas and brush their teeth. Next, the mother would read a story or two and the kids would make their last trip to the bathroom. Those who stayed in bed the night before, got a piggy-back ride to bed from mom. Finally, they ended the routine with nightly prayers and a bedtime song. Now, this routine didn't work perfectly every night and there were occasional activities, telephone calls, or meetings that interrupted the schedule. But those were the exceptions, not the rule. In general, the kids could expect some time with their parent at the end of the day and bedtime problems decreased measurably.

Kids like structure. It helps them learn responsible behaviors. They know what they should do and when they should do it. For kids, consistency and daily routines reduce problems and confusion. For parents, consistency and daily routines help reduce the hassles and makes a home run much smoother.

Notes

Chapter 9

Staying Calm

Many parents tell us that the biggest challenge they face in dealing with their child's problem behaviors is staying calm. We all know there are times when our kids are going to make us upset and angry. Kids can be sarcastic, defiant, rebellious, and possibly violent. Parents have to prepare themselves for times like these and learn to keep their cool.

Please understand that we are not saying you won't get angry. That's impossible, maybe even unhealthy, since anger is a basic human emotion. We are simply saying that blowing your top over your child's behavior can make situations worse. The way we look at it, anger is only one letter away from "danger."

When we ask other parents what they do when they are angry, they typically say they yell or swear at their kids. Some say that they hit something, and throw or kick things. Many parents were totally convinced that these angry responses worked to show their kids they "meant business." And they were right. These responses did temporarily stop the problem behavior. But, what did their children learn? They learned to yell, hit, and throw or kick things when they are upset. As these parents went through our Common Sense Parenting classes, they learned to stay calm in tense situations. And, they reported the following results: 1) their kids' temper tantrums or problem behaviors stopped sooner; 2) their kids' problem behavior did not last as long and wasn't as severe; and 3) the parents felt better about the way they handled the situation. In one particular case, a stepparent told us, "You know, that 'calm' thing really works. My son used to run away frequently. Usually, it was after he did something wrong and I'd get mad at him. Then we'd start arguing and he'd leave. After I learned how to stay calm and not go bonkers, we both stayed more calm and were able to work things out without him running away."

Of course, staying calm was just one of the effective changes this man made in his parenting style. But staying calm was only the first step. He learned that all of those other times, his anger got in the way of what he wanted to teach his stepson. As he learned to remain calm, he was able to put his other parenting skills to work. This led to a dramatic, positive change in the relationship between this man and his stepson.

In this chapter we lay out a plan for staying calm. There are three steps in developing your "Staying Calm" plan: 1) identify what your kids do that gets you upset; 2) identify what you are doing or feeling that signals you are getting upset; and 3) decide what you are going to do differently in the future.

Step One: The Storm Before the Calm

Knowing what makes us angry is the first step in being able to respond calmly to our kids' problem behaviors. Typically, kids are able to push our buttons, say the words, or do the actions that get under our skin. You know what we mean. It's when you're dead tired and you ask your kids to help with the dishes. They roll their eyes and moan about being asked to do all the work. Next, they argue about never getting to do anything. By then, you're ready to blow your stack!

When we ask parents what gets them upset, they often respond with, "I hate it when he talks to me that way," or "Her moodiness drives me crazy!" What these parents are missing are the specific behaviors that irritate and upset them. If parents can specify which children's behaviors occur just before they get angry, they'll be more likely to reduce the intensity and severity of their own response and also help their children's behavior improve.

On a separate piece of paper, list the specific behaviors that your kids have done that resulted in you losing your temper.

Pay attention to what your kids said, what they did, what voice tone they used, and so on. Also, it will help to identify the situations in which these behaviors occur. For example, did this annoying behavior occur after you gave them an instruction, corrected them, or asked them to help around the house? Or did it happen at a certain time of day, such as, before school or before bedtime. The more specific you make the list, the more likely it is that you'll be able to stay calm when facing these situations in the future.

Step Two: Warning Signs

There are a whole series of feelings that flood our bodies when we start to get upset. Our behavior also changes. At these times, how you deal with these feelings makes all the difference in what you do or say. If you lose control, you're likely to make the situation worse by hurting your kids' feelings or saying and doing things you'll later regret. In other words, rarely does anything good happen when you get upset with your kids and lose self-control.

We all have little signals that show we're getting angry. Recognizing these "red flags" allows us to think before we act. It's much easier to work our way through a problem when we can remain calm.

What are your "red flags?" Does your heart race or face get flushed? Do you clench your teeth, make a fist, or feel your muscles tighten? Do you talk faster or louder or start pointing and making abrupt movements? Take some time to think about the early warning signs that indicate you're beginning to get upset. Before you can change how you respond to your kids, you have to know exactly what your anger signs are. On the sheet of paper where you listed your kids' behavior, write down the things you do when you're beginning to get angry.

Step Three: Make a Plan

Now, let's take a look at how you can use these signals to help you stay calm in tense situations with your children. Here's how we taught other parents to put this information into practice. What we're going to do in this example is combine:

1. Your child's problem behaviors, and
2. Your early warning signals, with
3. A way of staying calm that works for you.

The following is an example of one parent's "Staying Calm" plan:

> The next time Jasbir talks back to me and refuses to go to bed (child's problem behaviors), and I start feeling my heart pound (my warning signals), I will take a deep breath and let it out slowly before I correct him (what I will do to stay calm).

Staying calm wasn't easy for this parent at first. She had to work at it. But the more she concentrated on her plan, the more successful she was at staying calm. She said she felt better about the way she interacted with her son and almost felt a sense of pride in maintaining her self-control.

Here are some ways that other parents have told us that they calm down in tense situations:

"I count to 10 – very slowly. I concentrate on doing that regardless of what my son is yelling."

"I put my hands in my pockets. I tend to talk with my hands, especially when I'm angry. Before I learned to do this, I think my daughter thought I was going to hit her. I wasn't, but she viewed my behavior as a threat."

"I sit down. If I'm standing, I begin to tremble. Sitting calms me for some reason. I can still tell my child what he's doing wrong, but I say it a lot more calmly."

"I take a deep breath and let it out slowly. This kind of serves as a safety valve to me. It's like I'm letting steam out of my body."

"I just leave the situation for awhile. I go in another room until I can handle myself. I figure if my kid's that mad, taking a little time to regain my control won't hurt anything. I can deal with it a lot better that way. Sometimes, he even calms down by the time I get back."

"This may sound crazy, but I wear a rubber band on my wrist and snap the band whenever I feel like I'm getting upset. That's a signal to myself that I'd better calm down."

"I used to get so upset with my 15-year-old that I would have to go outside for a walk to calm down. I couldn't do this every time, but it's been helpful on many occasions."

"I call someone like my best friend or my sister. By talking about the situation, I can go back in and deal with it more calmly."

"I sit down and on paper write about how upset I am. Sometimes, I can't even read what I've written. That's not as important as the fact that I'm not taking it out on my son. When I calm down, I'm always surprised at how upset I got at such a little thing."

On the same piece of paper that you listed Step One and Step Two, put the finishing touches on it by writing a plan for yourself. Parents tell us that when they write out their plan, they are more likely to remember it and use it during a real situation.

It might look something like this:

The next time my child (child's problem behavior)
and I start (my warning signals)
I will (what I will do to stay calm)

Tips for Staying Calm

Learning to control your negative reactions will take some time. Don't get discouraged if you lose your temper every now and then. Here are some tips that have helped other parents:

Practice positive thinking. If you find yourself thinking negative thoughts, interrupt those thoughts. Say "Stop it!" to yourself. Then refocus with positive thoughts. It helps you keep your self-control and work through whatever problem you're dealing with.

Here are some examples of positive thinking that other parents have used:

"Relax. Take it easy."
"I am going to help my child."
"Take it slowly."
"I'm a good parent and I can do this."
"It's going to get better. It just takes time."

You will find that the more frequently you use positive thinking, the better you will feel about yourself and your role as a parent. Even if you don't see any immediate change in your child's behavior, you can certainly prevent the problem from getting worse.

Negative, self-defeating thoughts always lead to more problems. By thinking positive thoughts, you not only learn to control your emotions, but also are able to better concentrate on the task at hand – teaching your children better ways to behave.

Don't take what your child says personally. This may be very difficult when your child is calling you every name in the book. You must convince yourself that the reason is because your child hasn't yet acquired the skills necessary to deal with anger or frustration. Don't react when you get called a name or when you are accused of being a rotten parent. Learn how to let negative, angry comments bounce off you and the effectiveness of your teaching will increase. If you are concerned about something your child says, use a problem-solving approach after he or she has calmed down.

Use the "take five" rule. Instead of blurting out an angry response, take five minutes to think about what is happening. It is remarkable how that "cooling off" period can help a person regain self-control and put things in perspective. Simply leaving the situation sometimes can help to "defuse" a volatile situation.

Focus on behavior instead of what you think are the reasons for your child's misbehavior. Don't look for motives; instead, deal with the way your child is acting. You can drive yourself batty trying to figure out reasons for your child's negative behavior. After the problem is solved, then take the time to talk to your child about what happened and why.

If you get angry and say or do something you regret, go back and say you're sorry. This models for your children what to do when they make a mistake. Apologize, say what you did wrong, and what you're going to do differently next time. Some parents worry about apologizing to their kids because they think it causes them to lose some of their parental control. We've found apologizing helps kids realize that we all, young and old alike, make mistakes. Apologizing makes parents more "human" too. Kids sometimes feel that parents are always right, no matter what happens. Admitting a mistake is the responsible thing to do. It's best to apologize and do your best not to let it happen again.

Staying calm does not mean you are totally passive. There are times when you will raise your voice – but it should be a firm, no-nonsense voice tone. And, the words you use are specific descriptions, not judgments, or put-downs, or negative feelings. Staying calm means you don't react to misbehavior in an angry, aggressive manner.

Summary

It's not easy to stay calm when you're dealing with your kids' negative behavior. But parents report that it's one of the most important parts of parenting. If you can stay calm, you'll be much more likely to teach your kids positive ways of handling problems. Identify what your kids do that makes you angry. Also, look at your own early warning signals that tell you

you're getting upset and develop a plan for staying calm. Finally, use your plan for staying calm to help you deal with those emotionally intense situations with your kids.

Notes

Chapter 10

Corrective Teaching

Children are constantly testing limits. In many respects, this is healthy. Testing limits is one way they learn and grow and find out about the world around them. However, when kids continually test the limits set by parents, it can cause problems for the whole family. Corrective Teaching is our method of dealing with these problems. In fact, many parents can't wait for us to present this section in our Common Sense Parenting classes. When we ask them to list problems they face, we get quick reactions. Here are some of the things they've said:

"I always have to ask two or three times whenever I want my kids to do something."

"It seems like my kids argue all the time. And, about the dumbest things. They just pick, pick, pick at one another until one of them gets mad."

"I can't get my kids to stop watching TV. They don't do their homework. They don't help out. They just want to watch TV."

"I can't get them to help with the dishes unless I threaten to take away a privilege."

"When I ask my son about his homework, he says it's done or he left it at school. Sooner or later, he gets a bad slip from school."

"It's to the point where I don't even look in my kid's rooms, let alone ask the kids to clean them. Those rooms are disaster areas."

"My daughter leaves her toys all over the house. I just feel like selling all of them at a garage sale."

Well, you get the picture. One parent summed up the frustration many parents feel when she said, "What can I do? I've had it! I feel like all I do is yell all day. They think I'm an ogre but I can't get them to do a thing!"

This parent, like most concerned parents, was looking for a constructive, effective way to respond to her child's constant misbehavior.

We taught her a four-step process called Corrective Teaching.

When to Use Corrective Teaching

Generally, you use Corrective Teaching when your kids are doing something they shouldn't do. Here are some specific situations where Corrective Teaching may be used:

1. When your kids don't follow your instructions.
2. When they are doing something that could result in harm to them or others.
3. When they refuse to accept criticism.
4. When they argue with your decisions.
5. When they don't accept responsibility for their behavior.
6. When they lie.
7. When they don't let you know where they are.

There are many other situations when Corrective Teaching can be used. As a general rule, whenever you see something you want to correct in their behavior, use Corrective Teaching. Now, let's see how we can use it to respond to specific problems.

How to Use Corrective Teaching

Corrective Teaching combines clear messages with consequences and practice to help parents respond to problem behavior. Corrective Teaching is similar to the parenting skills in the previous chapters. As one parent put it, "Corrective

Teaching gives me a plan for responding to my kids' misbehavior. I was doing some of it sometimes – like giving consequences – but I really wasn't teaching. So my kids never learned what to do. They only learned what I didn't like."

Corrective Teaching gives parents a process for responding to problem behaviors and teaching alternative behaviors.

The Steps of Corrective Teaching

- ***Stop the problem behavior***
- ***Give a consequence***
- ***Describe what you want***
- ***Practice what you want***

Kids are going to misbehave. That's part of being a kid. Parents need to be prepared to teach their kids what they can do instead of misbehaving. That's part of being a parent. Corrective Teaching gives parents a plan for responding to these routine misbehaviors.

Let's look at an example of Corrective Teaching. Your daughter just came home 30 minutes past her curfew. She didn't let you know she was going to be late. You ask her why she wasn't on time and she tells you that her friends didn't want to leave the party so early. You use Corrective Teaching:

Stop the problem behavior
"Deepa, you came home 30 minutes late and didn't let me know that you weren't going to be on time."

Give a consequence
"Tomorrow night you have to be home an hour earlier."

Describe what you want
"When you're going to be late, call and let me know. Depending on the situation, you can either stay later if your ride is leaving later or I'll come and get you. But you have to call and let me know that you'll be late. Okay?"

Practice what you want

Mom - "Now, how would you handle the situation next time?"
Deepa - "I'd call and ask you if I can stay later."
Mom - "Okay, I'll probably ask you, 'Why?' What would you say then?"
Deepa - "Well, I'd tell you that Malini isn't leaving for another half hour and that she was going to give me a ride."
Mom - "And I'd probably say you could stay and that when you get home, we'll talk about arranging rides that will get you home on time. See, if you call, we know that you're safe. You stay out of trouble. And sometimes it works out where you can stay later."

Things might not go this smoothly for you every time you use Corrective Teaching but this example gives you a picture of how the steps are used. If your children start arguing, yelling, or their behavior gets worse in other ways, then read the next chapter, which gives you a way to respond to emotionally intense situations with your children.

Here's a brief overview of the Corrective Teaching steps.

Stop the Problem Behavior

Stopping the problem behavior helps focus your children's attention on what you are saying. Start by calmly getting their attention and giving them clear instructions such as, "Stop fighting and sit down in the chair," or "Please hang up the telephone now." Eliminate as many distractions as possible and get at their eye level. You want them to concentrate on you and your teaching. If the problem behavior has already stopped, then just describe the problem behavior. For example, "Dinesh before I left for the store, I asked you to pick up your clothes and put away the clean dishes. Instead, you have been playing video games."

Give a Consequence

Consequences help children make the connection between what they do and what happens as a result of their actions.

Negative consequences, such as removing a privilege or adding a chore, reduce the frequency or severity of the behaviors they follow. In other words, if we want Dinesh to spend less time playing video games and more time following instructions, we would say something like, "Since you didn't do what I asked, you can fold a load of laundry after picking up your clothes and putting away the dishes. All this has to be done before you play video games again." Remember to use the smallest consequence that will work. Also, when you pick a consequence, remember the characteristics that make them effective: importance, immediacy, frequency, size, and contingency.

Describe what you want

This is the same step you used in Effective Praise and Preventive Teaching. Be clear, specific, and stick to describing what behavior you want your children to do in place of the problem behavior. Use the skills described in Chapter 16, "Social Skills," to help you identify what you want your kids to do instead of their misbehavior. In our example, Dinesh didn't follow his mom's instructions to do a couple of chores. His mom might say, "Okay, Dinesh any time I ask you to do something, I want you to tell me that you'll do it and get started on it right away."

Practice what you want

Practice. Practice. Practice. Each time your children practice doing things right, you are increasing their chances for success and decreasing the likelihood that you will see that problem behavior in the future. You give them one more opportunity to learn something new. Practice helps them remember just what they can do to avoid problems and get things right. For example, Mom might say, "Dinesh, show me how you'll get the chores done next time." And Dinesh, might slowly answer, "All right," and shuffle off to get started on his chores. Mom says, "Thanks for getting started right away. You just practiced how to follow instructions. Now, you'll get finished right away and get back to your games sooner."

Examples of Corrective Teaching

Here are some examples of Corrective Teaching. A father tells his daughter to begin her homework. When he comes back in the room, his daughter is watching TV.

Stop the problem behavior
"Monica, please turn off the TV. I know you like to watch TV but you're supposed to be doing your homework."

Give a consequence
"Since you were watching TV instead of doing your homework, leave the TV off for one hour after you finish your assignments."

Describe what you want
"When I ask you to get started on your homework, I want you to stop what you're doing and begin your homework right away." If you do this, you can get back to what you were doing as soon as you have completed your homework.

Practice what you want
"Now here's a chance for you to show me you can do what we've talked about. You've done a good job of listening so far. Now it's time for you to get your books and start studying."

A five-year-old is pestering her father while he is on the telephone. The father has excused himself from the call and is sitting down to get at eye level with his daughter.

Stop the problem behavior
"Alisha, please sit up here on the chair. While I was talking on the phone you kept repeating, 'Daddy, I want more peanut butter.'"

Give a consequence
"Because you interrupted me while I was on the phone, want you to sit on your chair for two minutes."

(With young children, parents report that they find it helpful to have the child sit on the chair first. After the child sits for the required time, the parent tells the child what to do in future situations. There is a more detailed description of Time-Out and its use with younger children in Chapter 5, "Negative Consequences.")

Describe what you want
"When you want something and I'm on the phone, please wait until I hang up. Okay? Then I can hear what you say and give you an answer."

Practice what you want
"Let's pretend that I'm on the phone. Look up and see me on the phone and then go back to playing until I hang it up... All right! Thanks for waiting. Let's get that peanut butter now."

Helpful Hints

Remain calm. Easy to say, but not always easy to do. Parents consistently tell us this is one of the most important pieces of the puzzle. Sometimes, kids misbehave so darn often that parents respond angrily. Or, the behavior itself is so annoying that parents react abruptly or negatively. Please remember – stop, think about what you need to do, calm yourself, and proceed with Corrective Teaching. You are much more likely to effectively change your child's behavior when you do.

Stick to one issue. Most kids are masters at getting parents sidetracked. Some kids can get parents so far off the topic that they forget what the topic is. Familiar lines such as the following are particularly effective:

"You don't love me!"
"My friends don't have to do that. Their parents are nice."
"I don't want to talk about that. And, you can't make me."

"You can take away anything you want. I just don't care."
"I can't wait until I'm a parent. I'll do nice things for my kids."

These types of comments often go straight to a parent's heart. We've all wanted to respond by telling our kids something sarcastic like, "Then go live with your friend's 'nice parents'," or by listing all of the good things we do for our kids. However, now is not the time for either. Stick with what you want to teach. Let your kids know that if they really want to talk about other topics, they can bring them up after the main issue (their misbehavior) is resolved.

Provide a chance to earn something back. If your child is attentive and works to make up for the misbehavior, and you are pleased with the attempt, don't hesitate to give some part of the consequence back. For example, during Corrective Teaching, you took away one hour of TV time because your son and daughter were arguing. After you finished, both of the children apologized and said they would work together to clean the dishes. If they cooperate, you could give back up to half of the TV time they lost. Doing this allows you to give them a positive consequence for working on the problem. This is an effective way to teach children to make up for mistakes or misbehaviors.

Be consistent. While the world around us is constantly changing, it helps kids to have some consistency in their lives. This means that if the kids' bedtime is 9:30 each night, then they should be in bed on time. If they are, let them know it. Use Effective Praise and maybe some creative rewards. If they are late to bed, use Corrective Teaching and eliminate the rewards. The more consistent you are, the more consistent your children will be.

Be flexible. Just when we said to be consistent, we throw you a curve and talk about flexibility. What we mean is that you should consistently use Corrective Teaching, but you can vary the way you use it. No one knows your child better than you. If you think that your daughter will learn more if you put the consequence at the end of the teaching sequence, then give it a try. If it works, then keep using Corrective Teaching that way. If it doesn't work, then try another way.

Use consequences. Some parents feel uncomfortable using consequences, even as the last step in the teaching sequence. It is true that some behavior may change over time when parents use Corrective Teaching without the "consequence" step because the time the parent spends teaching is enough of a consequence to change the behavior. On the other hand, consequences usually increase the effectiveness of your teaching. Consequences increase the likelihood that children will make the connection between what they did and what they get to do. They come to understand that their behavior has an effect on others as well as themselves.

Summary

Think about one of your child's typical misbehaviors. Then figure out what you would say for each Corrective Teaching step. Practice it in front of the mirror a few times before using it with one of your kids. Mirrors are a friendly place to start; they don't talk back as much as children. Once you've seen and heard yourself, and you feel like you're willing to give it a try with your child, go to it. Practice leads to confidence and confidence leads to success.

It works. Parents who take the time to use each of the steps of Corrective Teaching are amazed at how it helps to change problem behaviors. Their attitude about parenting takes an about-face. They don't hesitate to correct their children's misbehavior and teach them a better way to behave. Parenting certainly is no less of a challenge, but now they're able to see constructive results. They take the opportunity to teach whenever possible; they use Corrective Teaching comfortably and confidently. Corrective Teaching will work for you, too.

Notes

Chapter 11

Teaching Self-Control

"You're a complete idiot. I hate you!"
"Get outta my face!"
"No way! I ain't gonna do it, and you can't make me!"

One of the more frustrating aspects of parenting is dealing with your child when he or she becomes angry or defiant or simply refuses to do what you ask. The child may be yelling, hitting, arguing, throwing objects, or threatening you. Your child's behavior can make you feel powerless, emotionally drained, or just plain furious.

If you have ever felt like this, you're not alone. All parents experience situations like this at one time or another. In fact, some parents face these situations frequently. One thing is certain however: Kids must learn that negative, aggressive behavior is not acceptable. It is harmful to them and others. The sooner kids learn to control their actions, the more they will benefit. Our method has helped parents teach their children a better way to respond when they get upset. We call it "Teaching Self-Control."

There are two key parts to Teaching Self-Control: getting your child calmed down and follow-up teaching. We'll talk about each part in detail, but first let's take a brief look at what often happens when a child yells at the parent or refuses to do what was asked.

In these situations, a child is certainly not interested in, and in some cases, not capable of discussing the situation rationally. A great deal of talking by the parent does little to improve the situation. Often, the more the parent talks, the louder the child yells. The more the child yells, the louder the parent talks – until the parent is yelling, too. This unpleasant exchange of words and actions continues to intensify until someone decides that the argument is too painful and drops out. It can be the parent, who walks out of the room in disgust and anger. Or, it can be the child, who stomps off to the bedroom and slams the door shut. In either case, the problem has gotten worse, not better. If you've had to deal with a situation like this, you know how helpless a parent feels at these emotionally intense times.

The steps of Teaching Self-Control give parents a way to stop the yelling or arguing before it gets harmful, before problems get worse. Teaching Self-Control gives parents a method for helping their kids identify how they're feeling and learn how to deal with these behaviors in ways that are helpful, not hurtful.

When to Use Teaching Self-Control

Basically, parents report that they use Teaching Self-Control in two types of situations:

1. When their child misbehaves and will not respond to Corrective Teaching; instead, the child continues or the misbehavior gets worse.

2. When their child "blows up" – a sudden and intense emotional outburst – and refuses to do anything that the parents ask.

Think of the last time your children got upset when you corrected their behavior or asked them to do something. What triggered their negative behavior? What exactly did they do? How did you respond? Looking back at past "blow-ups" can help you plan for how you will deal with them in the future. One way to prevent blow-ups is to use your plan for staying calm (Chapter 9) and the steps of Teaching Self-Control. These steps are described on the following pages.

The Steps of Teaching Self-Control

The goals of Teaching Self-Control are: 1) to help you and your children calm down during emotionally intense interactions, and 2) to teach your children how to control their behavior when they get upset.

The first part of Teaching Self-Control is geared toward decreasing the intensity of your interaction so that both of you can work to resolve the disagreement.

The second part of Teaching Self-Control is Follow-up Teaching. It gives you an opportunity to teach your child some acceptable ways of behaving – some options – when your child is upset. Like the other skills you have learned, Teaching Self-Control emphasizes giving clear descriptions of your child's behaviors, using consequences, and teaching your child the correct behavior.

Part One: Calming Down

- ***Describe the problem behavior***
- ***Give clear instructions***
- ***Allow time to calm down***

Part Two: Follow-Up Teaching

- ***Describe what your child could do differently next time***
- ***Practice what your child can do next time***
- ***Give a consequence***

Teaching Self-Control gives both you and your kids a chance to calm down after tempers have flared. Allowing time to calm down before continuing your teaching increases the likelihood that your kids will have learned to share their feelings in constructive ways. Let's take a look at the steps of Teaching Self-Control and an explanation of each.

Part One: Calming Down

Describe the Problem Behavior

Briefly tell your child exactly what he or she is doing wrong. We emphasize "briefly" here. Your child is not always interested in listening to what you have to say at this time, so saying a lot won't help. You will have time to describe the problem in detail once your child settles down. Remember to be clear and specific with what you do say. You should talk in a calm, level voice tone. Don't speak rapidly or try to say too much. For example, "Mohit, you're yelling at me and pacing around the room," gives the child a clear message about what he is doing.

Parents often say judgmental things when they dislike their child's behavior. They say things such as, "Quit acting like a baby," or "You have a lousy attitude." But even though you don't like the behavior, using vague or judgmental statements serves only to fuel the emotional fire in your child. We suggest that you simply describe what your child is doing wrong without becoming angry, sarcastic, or accusatory.

It also helps to use empathy when your child is upset or angry. As we said earlier, empathy means that you show understanding for the other person's feelings. For instance, you might say, "I know you are upset right now. And, I know you're unhappy with what happened." This starts the teaching sequence positively and shows your child that you really do care about his or her feelings. Plus, using empathy often helps you focus on your child's behavior rather than your own emotions.

Earlier, we asked you to think of the last time your children got upset when you corrected their behavior or asked them to do something. In that situation, were you satisfied that your descriptions of your child's behavior were clear and specific? Were they brief? Could you have used an empathy statement? Did you use words that your child easily understood? How could you have used the information we just discussed to improve your descriptions? Thinking about past incidents can help you learn how to best apply these techniques in the future.

Give Clear Instructions

The purpose of this step is to tell your child exactly what he or she needs to do to begin calming down. Give simple instructions like, "Please go to your room or sit on the porch and calm down." Or, make calming statements to your child like, "Take a few deep breaths and try to settle down." As when describing the problem behavior, keep your words to a minimum. Don't give too many instructions or repeat them constantly; the child could perceive this as lecturing or badgering. Simple, clear options keep the focus on having your child regain self-control.

It is very important that parents practice these first two steps. The emphasis is on using clear messages to help calm your child. Practicing this skill is time worth investing. Besides giving your child important information about his or her behavior, clear messages help keep you on track.

Allow Time to Calm Down

Parents tell us that this is the most important step in the whole process. If parents remain calm, it increases the likelihood that their child will calm down faster. Parents also tell us that remembering this step has helped them focus on their child's behavior. Simply saying, "We both need a little time to calm down. I'll be back in a few minutes," can be very effective. Remember, sometimes giving your child a little "space" helps your child "save face."

As parents take the time to calm down, they can think of what they are going to teach next. This also allows the child to make a decision – to continue misbehaving or to calm down.

Come back to the child as often as necessary. Ask questions like, "Can we talk about what happened?" or "Are you calmed down enough to talk to me?"

Move to the next phase when your child is able to answer you in a reasonably calm voice and is paying attention to what you say. You're not going to have the happiest child at this point, but it's important that he or she can talk without losing self-control again.

Take your time. Give descriptions and instructions as needed. Most of all, be calm and in control of what you say and do.

Part Two: Follow-Up Teaching

Describe What Your Child Could Do Differently Next Time

Describe what your child can do differently next time. Explain another way to express frustration or anger. Kids have to learn that when they "blow up" every time something doesn't go their way, it leads to more negative consequences. This is an opportunity to explain the prompts you gave in Step Two and to encourage your child to remember how to calm down.

We teach many of our parents to rely on the "Instead of..." phrase. It goes like this:

> "Instead of yelling and running out the door, the next time you get upset, please tell me you're mad and ask if you can go to your room to calm down."
>
> "Instead of swearing, why don't you ask if you can sit on the porch until you are ready to talk about it."

The purpose of this phrase is to teach kids what they can do the next time they get upset. Parents can teach their children to recognize when they are beginning to get upset. They also can teach their children to say something like, "I'm getting mad. Can I have some time to calm down?"

Once your children calm down, they can talk about the circumstances that triggered their anger and talk with you about a solution. If parents and kids can learn to talk about how they feel in these situations, they will be much more successful attacking the problem rather than attacking each other.

Practice What Your Child Can Do Next Time

Now that your child knows what to do, it's important that he or she knows how to do it. By practicing, you are more likely to see the behavior you want the next time your child starts to get upset.

After the practice is over, let your child know what was done correctly and what needs improvement. Be as positive as you can be, especially if your child is making an honest effort to do what you ask.

Give a Consequence

This is a crucial part of Teaching Self-Control. If there is a common mistake made by the parents we work with, it is that they forget to give a consequence. Some comment that they were so pleased to have the yelling stop that giving a consequence didn't cross their minds. Other parents have told us that they just didn't have the heart to give a consequence because they didn't want to upset their child any more than he already was. Sometimes, after the situation is all over, parents want to ease up, or their children convince them to forget it altogether. These feelings are understandable but they may not make a difference in changing a child's behavior. Please remember that consequences help change behavior; use them.

We emphasize that you consistently use a negative consequence at the end of each Teaching Self-Control interaction. If you have given an appropriate negative consequence, follow through with it. Kids have to learn not to blow up or throw tantrums when things don't go the way they wanted. They can't use these behaviors in school and still get a good education. They can't use them on the job and stay employed. And most likely, they won't keep friends for very long if they can't control their tempers. As parents, we need to teach them how to respond in less harmful ways when they get upset. Consequences increase the effectiveness of your teaching, and the whole process of Teaching Self-Control helps your kids learn better ways of behaving.

Example of Teaching Self-Control

Let's take a look at an example of Teaching Self-Control. Here's the situation: You have just told your 10-year-old son that he can't go over to his friend's house because he hasn't finished cleaning his room. He yells, "That's so stupid! I hate you! You never let me do anything!" Then, he runs to his room screaming and cussing.

Part One: Calming Down

Describe the problem behavior

- Describe what happened or is happening.
- Clearly tell the child what he is doing wrong.

"I know you wanted to go to your friend's house, but you are yelling and swearing."

Give clear instructions

- Describe what you want him to do.
- Give options for calming down.

"Please stop yelling and either go to your room or stay out here and sit on the couch. Take a deep breath and do your best to calm down."

Allow time to calm down

- Give each of you a chance to calm down. (Leave the area for a few minutes. Come back and ask your child if he is willing to talk.)
- Check for cooperative behavior.

"Can we talk about this now?" or "I can see that you're still upset. I'll be back in a few minutes."

When your child is following your instructions and is willing to talk with you about the problem, move from the Calming Down phase to Follow-Up Teaching.

Part Two: Follow-Up Teaching

Describe what your child could do differently next time

- Think of a better way your child can react when he gets upset. Describe what he can do differently.

"Let's look at what you can do the next time you get upset. What I'd like you to do is let me know that you are getting upset and ask me if you can go to your room and calm down."

Practice what your child can do next time

- Practice increases the chance that your child will learn what to do next time.

"Give that a try. I'm going to tell you that you can't go out and play. What should you do? Okay, let's try it."

- Let him know how he practiced.

"Great! You told me you're getting mad and asked me if you could go to your room. And, you asked me in a nice voice tone. Thanks a lot."

Give a consequence

- Help prevent the problem from occurring again.

"Remember, there are consequences for yelling and swearing. Tonight, you'll have to do the dishes and sweep the floor after dinner."

In real-life situations, your child probably won't cooperate this quickly. He or she may go from arguing and swearing to being calm, and then suddenly start arguing again. Some kids have a lot of stamina when they're upset so it's best to realize it could take awhile before the problem is resolved. There also may be other distractions you will have to deal with in these situations; for example, your other kids need something, the phone rings, the soup is boiling over on the stove, and so on. Interactions with your child do not occur in a void; other things are always taking place that affect your behavior. Continue teaching. In these instances, use the skills you learned in the "Staying Calm" chapter, and adapt the teaching steps and your teaching style to the situation. Stick to simple descriptions and instructions, continue to use empathy, and stay calm.

Helpful Hints

Stay on task. Don't lose sight of what you're trying to teach. Implement all of the steps of Teaching Self-Control. Concentrating on your child's behavior is much easier when you have a framework to follow. Teaching

Self-Control gives you that framework. It helps you stay calm and avoid arguments that take you away from what you want to teach.

Your children may try to argue with what you say or call you names. They may say you don't love them or tell you how unfair you are. They may say things to make you feel guilty or angry or useless. Expect these statements but don't respond to them. If you get caught up in all of these side issues, you lose sight of your original purpose – to teach your child self-control. And, you can lose sight of the original problem and how you need to deal with it. If you find yourself responding to what your child is saying, remember to use a key phrase – "We'll talk about that when you calm down." Staying on task ensures that you won't start arguing or losing your temper.

Be aware of your physical actions. These times can be emotionally explosive. You don't want to encourage any physical retaliation from your child and you cannot be seen as a threat. Some parents find that sitting helps calm the situation quickly. When they stand up – particularly fathers – they tend to be more threatening. Any action viewed as aggressive will only make matters worse and lessen the likelihood that your child will calm down.

Pointing your index finger, putting your hands on your hips, scowling, leaning over your child, and raising a fist are all examples of physical actions that tend to increase tension in these volatile situations. Try your best to avoid these gestures. Keep your hands in your pockets, cross them over your chest – find something to do with them other than waving them at your child.

Plan consequences in advance. Think of appropriate negative consequences beforehand, especially if losing self-control is a problem for your child. Making decisions when your stomach's churning can lead to huge consequences that you can't follow through with.

Find time when your child is not upset to explain to her what the consequence will be the next time she argues and fights with you. For example, "Sarah, when I tell you 'No,' sometimes you want to argue with me. Then you get real mad and start yelling. From now on, if you do this, you will lose your phone privileges for two nights." Then explain to Sarah why she needs to accept decisions and why she shouldn't argue or scream. Possibly, knowing what the consequence will be may help your child think before losing self-control. And, as mentioned earlier, planned consequences help parents avoid giving unreasonable or harsh consequences that stem from being upset.

Follow up. As your child calms down and you complete the teaching sequence, numerous side issues can arise. For example, some situations may call for a problem-solving approach. Your child possibly doesn't have the knowledge or experience to deal with a certain situation. It may be very beneficial to take the time to help find solutions.

Other situations may call for a firm, emphatic ending to Teaching Self-Control. You may want to indicate that the child's behavior is clearly unacceptable and that you're finished with the interaction: "Okay, we've practiced what to do. Now go in your brother's room and apologize to him."

Still other situations may call for an understanding approach. Some kids cry after an intense situation. They just don't know how to handle what they're feeling inside. Then you can say, "Let's sit down and talk about why you've been feeling so angry. Maybe I can help. At least, I can listen."

Whatever approach you take will be determined by your common sense and judgment. It depends entirely on how you feel about the situation and what you want to teach.

Earlier we mentioned that you shouldn't get sidetracked with all of the comments and issues that kids may bring up when they were angry. But that's only during the Teaching Self-Control process. It is important, after everyone's calmed down, to follow up on those statements that upset or concerned you. This is when you can find out the reasons behind the outburst.

Kids may make comments during these emotionally intense situations because they have found out that these words have worked before. They may have found out that they could avoid getting a consequence or avoid doing what was asked. In other situations, kids may make these comments because they sincerely don't know how to express their feelings in healthy ways. Sometimes, children tell their parents that they just made negative comments because they were mad. Other times, kids really do have concerns, or don't feel trusted. And still other times, kids won't have a clue why they said what they did.

When you have finished Teaching Self-Control and both you and your child are calm, it is often helpful to discuss some of these comments that your child made. Tell your child that you're concerned about what was said. Talk about trust. Ask your child to share feelings and opinions with you.

Regardless of why they made the comments, take time to hear what your children are saying. Whenever possible, implement the suggestions they make. By doing so, you will be opening the door to more constructive conversations with your children. You will also be reducing the likelihood that your children will express these feelings in destructive ways. Frequently, going through these rough times together form the tightest emotional bonds between you and your kids.

Summary

Parents must have a bountiful supply of patience if their kids have a problem with self-control. The wisest parents are those who realize that having their kids learn self-control is an ongoing process. It takes a long time. Don't try to rush the learning process; expecting too much too soon can create more problems than it solves. Be attentive to small accomplishments; praise even the smallest bit of progress your child makes. (And, while you're at it, give yourself a big pat on the back. Teaching self-control is a tough job.)

Look for small positive changes over time. Your child possibly will have fewer angry outbursts, or the outbursts won't last as long, or they won't have nearly the intensity they once had.

Teaching Self-Control helps parents and children break the painful argument cycle. When tension is greatest in the family, Teaching Self-Control gives everyone a constructive way to get problems resolved.

Notes

Chapter 12

Making Decisions

No matter what their age, kids are making decisions all the time.

A four-year-old watches his ball roll out into the street. What does he do?

A 10-year-old's friend asks if he can copy her homework. What does she do?

A 16-year-old is offered some beer at a party. What does he do?

In each situation, these kids have a choice to make. Kids frequently make decisions on the spur of the moment, sometimes without thinking. They tend to look at solutions to problems as black or white, all or nothing, yes or no, do it or don't do it. Kids also focus on the immediate situation and have difficulty looking ahead to see how a decision could affect them later.

So, how can parents prepare their children to make the best decisions?

The SODAS Method

We use a five-step problem-solving method called **SODAS®**. The principles are simple, yet this method is adaptable to many situations. The **SODAS** method accomplishes two goals.

First, it gives parents and children a process for solving problems and making decisions together.

Second, it helps parents teach children how to solve problems and make decisions on their own.

The **SODAS** method helps both children and adults think more clearly and make a decision based on sound reasoning.

SODAS stands for:

1. **S**ituation
2. **O**ptions
3. **D**isadvantages
4. **A**dvantages
5. **S**olution

Let's look at each step of the **SODAS** process.

Define the Situation

Before you can solve a problem, you need to know what the problem is. Defining the situation sometimes takes the greatest amount of time because children often use vague or emotional descriptions. Also, kids aren't always aware that a certain situation could cause problems. A four-year-old may think that running into the street to retrieve his soccer ball isn't a problem; he's only thinking about getting the ball back. He doesn't realize the dangers of his actions.

Other decisions may not involve obvious dangers, but they still may have drawbacks. Regardless, these are opportunities for your child to make a choice. Kids will have to decide how to spend their allowance, what kids to hang around with, or whether to go out for sports or get a job. They can quickly run through the **SODAS** process to make these daily decisions.

Tips for defining the situation:

- Ask specific, open-ended questions to determine the situation. Avoid asking questions that your child can answer with a one-word answer: "Yes," "No," "Fine," "Good," etc. Instead, ask questions such as, "What did you do then?" or "What happened after you said that?" These questions help you piece together what really occurred.
- Teach children to focus on the entire situation, not just part of it. For example, questions that identify who, what, when, and where help you get a clear picture of the whole situation.

- Summarize the information. Kids sometimes get so overwhelmed by the emotions surrounding a problem that they lose sight of what the actual problem is. State the problem in the simplest, most specific form. Ask your child if your summary of the situation is correct.

Options

Once you have a complete description of the situation, you can begin discussing options – the choices your child has. There usually are several options to each problem.

Unfortunately, kids frequently think of solutions in the form of "all or nothing" options. For example, a student gets a bad grade on a test and immediately wants to change classes because everything is "ruined." Or, a bully is picking on another kid so the solution is to gang up on the bully. It's common for kids to only see one solution to a problem, or take the first one that pops into their heads. Other times, they may see no options at all.

Your role as a parent is to get your child to think. Ask questions like, "Can you think of anything else you could do?" or "What else could solve the problem?" Consistently asking these questions helps your child learn a process to use when making decisions without your guidance.

Tips for identifying options:

- Let your child list good and bad options. It's a common tendency for parents to cut right to the chase and tell their kids what to do. But the purpose here is to get your child to think of ways to make a decision on his or her own.
- Choose no more than three options. Any more than that tends to get confusing. (Also, make sure at least one of the options is reasonable and has a chance for success.)
- Suggest options if your child is having trouble coming up with them. This way, kids learn that in many situations there is more than one option.

Disadvantages/Advantages

In this step, you discuss with your child the pros and cons of each option. This helps your child see the connection between each option and what could happen if that option is chosen.

Tips for reviewing disadvantages and advantages:

- Ask your child for his or her thoughts about each option. What's good about the option? What's bad about the option? Why would the option work? Why wouldn't the option work?
- Help your child come up with both disadvantages and advantages for every option. This will be easier for your child to do with certain options; he or she may not have the experience or knowledge to know possible outcomes for all options.

Solution

At this point, it is time to choose an option that would work best. Briefly summarize the disadvantages and advantages for each option and ask your child to choose the best one.

Tips for choosing a solution:

- Make sure that your child knows the options and the possible outcomes of each one. You're trying to help your child make an informed decision and establish a pattern for making future decisions.
- Some decisions are hard to make. If the decision doesn't need to be made immediately, let your child take some time for additional thought.

Final Thoughts

Parents usually have a lot of questions about **SODAS** and the types of situations in which it can be used. Here are some things to think about when using the **SODAS** method.

Sometimes kids pick options that don't sit too well with their parents. In general, if the decisions won't hurt anyone, and aren't illegal or contrary to your moral or religious beliefs, then let your kids make the choice and learn from their decision. For example, your son might insist that he wants to spend most of his money on a very expensive video game. You may not agree with his choice but it won't affect anyone but him (and his cash flow) if he decides to buy the game. Possibly, let him buy it and learn from the consequences. Perhaps he will enjoy the game so much he won't mind not having money for other activities. On the other hand, he might wish that he had not bought such an expensive game. We would suggest that you let your son know that if he wants money after he spent all of his, you will not give it to him. If he wants to work or do something to earn money, that's a different story. But don't let him off the hook by giving in to pleas for money. This is one way he'll learn to make good decisions about spending his money.

Occasionally, kids face options that are illegal, immoral, or harmful to themselves or others. In these cases, parents should clearly and firmly state their disapproval, repeat the disadvantages to that solution, and let their child know the consequences of making that choice. For example, if your 16-year-old daughter decides that she wants to drink when she's out with her friends, you can let her know that you won't tolerate her drinking and spell out all of the many dangers. Also, tell her what consequences you will give her if she decides to drink. Sometimes, despite all of our efforts, kids still make wrong decisions. When that occurs, it is necessary to follow through with the consequences you described. Then, help your child go back through the **SODAS** process and come up with more acceptable solutions.

While you should encourage your kids to make some decisions on their own, you need to let them know that you'll be there to help at any time. This includes supporting them as they implement the solution. If the solution does not work out the way the child planned, you will be there to offer support and empathy. You and your child can then return to the **SODAS** format to find another solution to the problem.

In situations where you think it will be helpful, have your child practice putting the solution in effect. Practice increases your child's confidence about the solution that has been chosen and improves the chances for success.

Finally, check with your child to see how the solution worked. Set a specific time to talk about this. This is an excellent opportunity for you to praise your child on following through with the decision. You also can look for additional solutions, if necessary.

Summary

If this type of problem-solving is new to you, begin with a small problem first. Give your kids time to feel comfortable with the process. Many kids don't have the patience to think things out. They become exasperated and "just want to get it over with." Don't let them make rash choices. Teach them to make good decisions.

SODAS is an excellent process for teaching your child how to make decisions. It is practical and can be applied to many different situations that your child may face. You can feel confident that you have given your child an effective, easy-to-use method for solving problems.

Notes

Chapter 13

Reaching Goals with Charts and Contracts

One effective way to change behavior is to use charts and contracts. Basically, charts and contracts are agreements between you and your kids that spell out what they will receive from you when they behave in certain ways. With charts and contracts, privileges are contingent on specific behaviors you want to see from your kids. Remember 'Grandma's Rule'? "When you finish cleaning your room, then you can go out and play." If you were to write this agreement, you would make a contract. Charts are illustrated contracts that show similar agreements.

Both charts and contracts have three main points: 1) specify the behavior your child needs to change, 2) specify what privileges can be earned, and 3) specify how long the agreement is in effect.

When to Use Charts and Contracts

Charts and contracts are valuable tools that help keep track of the agreement made between you and your kids. Specifically, you can use them:

When you want to focus on a particular problem behavior. A child may frequently complain when asked to do something, have tantrums, or be late for school in the morning.

When your child has a goal in mind. A child may want to work toward earning money for a new bike, to have later bedtimes, or to be allowed to use the car on weeknights.

When you have a particular goal you'd like your child to achieve. You may want your child to start a savings account, get more involved in school activities, mow the lawn regularly, or get a job.

In each of these situations, a chart or a contract could be used to monitor and record the progress made toward the goal you have in mind.

Contracts

Here's how a contract might work with a 15-year-old girl who wants a later curfew and her parents who want her to come home on time.

Shefali's Curfew Agreement

I, Shefali, agree to be home by 9 o'clock on Sunday through Thursday nights and by 10 o'clock on Friday and Saturday nights. I have to do this for two weeks in a row before I get a later weekend curfew. If I am late coming home, I lose going out the following night. My two weeks of coming home on time begin again the next time I go out.

We, Mom and Dad, agree to let Shefali stay out until 10:30 p.m. on Friday and Saturday nights when she comes home on time for two weeks in a row.

We will mark the calendar each night after Shefali comes home on time. This will continue for two weeks or until the contract is renegotiated.

____________________ __________

(Shefali's signature) (Date)

____

(Parents' signature)

Here's another example of a contract. In this situation, the parent and child discussed completing homework consistently in exchange for watching TV.

Ranvir's Read and Watch Agreement

I, Ranvir, will study for at least 1 hour every evening (Sunday through Thursday) before asking to watch TV. I will start my homework assignments at 5 o'clock each day. If they take longer than 1 hour, I will work on them until they're finished. I understand that if I don't do my homework, I don't get to watch TV.

I, Mom, will let Ranvir watch TV for one hour each night when he completes his homework as expected.

We will go over Ranvir's homework each night when he is finished. We will continue this contract for two weeks.

______________________________ ________________

(Ranvir's signature) (Date)

____

(Mom's signature)

Charts

Let's take a look at how a chart worked for Karan, 10, and his parents. Karan was interested in having later bedtimes, especially on weekends. Karan's parents wanted him to go to bed on time without arguing each night. They used the chart called "Karan's Bedtime Bonanza," shown on the next page, to help Karan go to bed on time.

Karan's bedtime on weeknights was 9 o'clock. Each weeknight that Karan went to bed on time without arguing he put a star on the corresponding stair. (It can be a stick figure, happy

Karan's Bedtime Bonanza

Weekday Bedtime is 9:00 p.m.

Each school night that I get to bed on time, I draw a stick figure on my chart. The number of times I get to bed on time tells me how late I can stay up on Friday and Saturday nights.

Friday and Saturday Bedtimes

1 day	9:15 p.m.
2 days	9:30 p.m.
3 days	9:45 p.m.
4 days	10:00 p.m.
5 days	10:30 p.m.

face, or whatever symbol your child likes to use.) The number of times Karan reached the goal determined how late he got to stay up on Friday and Saturday. The more nights he went to bed on time, the later he got to stay up on the weekend. So, going to bed on time without arguing on three of the five weeknights earned a 9:45 p.m. bedtime on Friday and Saturday. There was an incentive built in for getting to bed every night on time. He increased his weekend bedtime by yet another half hour by getting that fifth night.

While this was set up to help Karan get to bed on time, the same idea can be used for several different goals, such as, homework completion, being ready for school on time in the morning, helping others each day, keeping the bedroom clean, and so on. Any of these goals could use a similar chart to get the job done.

At the end of this chapter are several examples of charts that can be adapted for your children. Many parents enjoy coming up with creative charts for their kids. Some of the most creative designs have come from the kids themselves. Young children, in particular, love to get out the crayons and make a colorful chart. This is a positive way to get your child involved in the process and gives you one more thing to praise.

Tips for Successful Charts and Contracts

State the goal positively. Use "When you finish your homework, you can watch TV" instead of, "If you don't finish your homework, you don't get to watch TV." Either one of these can be true, but it's easier to reach a goal if you're working toward something positive.

Follow through on the agreement. Be sure to review your child's progress each day and provide encouragement to keep going. When your child reaches the goal, give what you promised. And, pile on the praise!

Make the goals specific and measurable. A goal of "completing homework each night" is easier to measure than "doing better in school." Likewise, it's easier to tell if your child is "offering to help Mom once a day" than "being more responsible." Being specific and clear lets you know when your child has reached the goal.

Keep the goals reasonable. Setting reachable goals is especially important when you are first introducing the idea of a chart or contract.

Make it fun. Charts and contracts are used to help kids reach goals and experience success. This will be more enjoyable if it's fun for you and your child. Make a big deal out of each day's progress and use lots of praise during the day when your child is working toward the goal.

Charts and contracts are a great way to help children see the successes they achieve. Charts and contracts also open lines of communication so parents and children reach goals together.

Summary

Identifying goals and planning together requires conversation between parent and child. For both to be winners, negotiation is necessary. The time spent setting up charts or contracts shows your children you care and are interested in helping them succeed.

Before kids get to do what they want, they have to keep their end of the bargain. Charts and contracts are simple, straight forward, and geared toward helping parents and children make improvements and get things accomplished.

Sameer's "S" Curve

Each time Mom finds me playing nicely with my sister, I get to color in a circle. When three circles are colored, I get the reward.

Behavior: Playing nicely with my sister.

Reward: Mom reads a book to me.

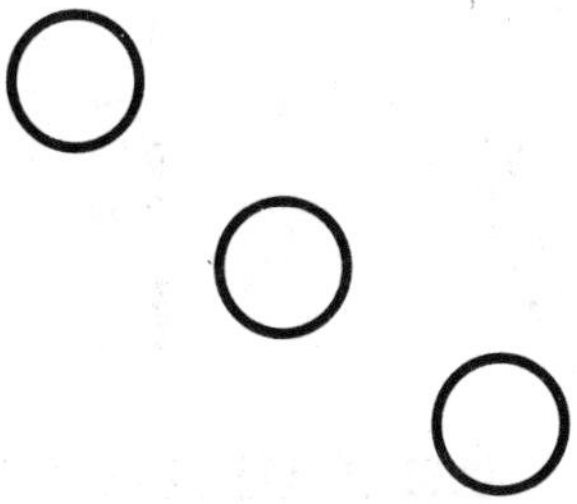

Reward: Play catch for 15 minutes with Mom.

Reward: Pick a snack.

Rahul's Rebound

Each day that I finish my homework, I get to color a basketball. On weekends, I get to color a ball if I read for 30 minutes. Each day that I color a ball, I get to shoot baskets outside with Mom for 15 minutes.

End of the Week Bonus

On Saturday, I get a bonus for having 4 or more balls colored during the week.

4 balls colored = grocery shopping on Saturday
5 balls colored = friends come over on Saturday
6 balls colored = bike ride on Sunday with Dad
7 balls colored = friends stay overnight on Saturday

Mahesh's Morning Stars

	Get Dressed 	Make Bed 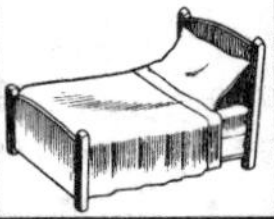	Eat Breakfast 	Brush Teeth 	Ready for School on Time 
Monday					
Tuesday					
Wednesday					
Thursday					
Friday					
Saturday					
Sunday					

Each day that I have 3 stars, I get to pick one of the following:

1. Call a friend on the phone.
2. Ride my bike.
3. Use special glass at dinner.

Each day that I have 4 stars, I get to pick two from this list or the 3-star list.

1. Go to bed 15 minutes later.
2. Call two friends on the phone.
3. Play a card game with Mom or Dad.

Each day that I have 5 stars, I get to pick three things to do from any list.

1. Go to bed 30 minutes later.
2. Have a friend over to play.
3. Go to a friend's house to play.

Saroj's On-Time Calendar

	Up on time 	To school on time	 Home from school on time	 To bed on time
Monday				
Tuesday				
Wednesday				
Thursday				
Friday				
Saturday				
Sunday				

I can earn 4 happy faces each day. The number of happy faces I have on my chart tells me what special things I get to do each day.

1 Happy Face = Piggyback ride to bed
2 Happy Faces = Bike ride plus above
3 Happy Faces = Checkers before bed plus above
4 Happy Faces = 15-minute later bedtime plus above

Notes

Chapter 14

Family Meetings

Families are busy. It's hard to find time to spend together. Work, school, sports, organizations, and other activities greatly affect the amount of time families can be together. Family Meetings can help busy families organize their time, share information, and make decisions.

Here are some things you can do during Family Meetings:

Coordinate schedules. Your kids can tell you what upcoming activities they have; they can plan for school or for playing with friends. You can ask important questions like who needs supplies, transportation, money, or materials for the week. A home operates better when information like this is shared. It certainly makes life easier for you when plans are made in advance.

Give praise. Family Meeting is an ideal time to praise each of your kids and to let everyone know about their achievements or accomplishments. Show your approval for improvements at school, for offers to help out around the house, or for getting along with another child. Let everyone know about attempts to solve problems. Think of creative ways for your kids to learn to praise one another. One parent we know starts each meeting by having everyone say something nice about the person sitting to the right. This is a positive way to get the meeting started.

Have family discussions. Here's a time for you and your kids to share information about all those other "things" going on in your lives. Give your kids a chance to talk about what happened in their school, what they discussed in class about local or world events, problems they're having with friends, and things they'd like to do as a family. You, too, get to share your opinion about these important issues. Be sure to bring some of your own "things" to discuss, like what you've been doing at work, current events, what's happening with other relatives, and your opinions of the latest fads or music. Family Meeting is a time to talk and listen, to share and discuss. This opportunity helps children develop their own views and beliefs by listening to the opinions of others. It can be fun, entertaining, and educational as it brings the family closer together.

Make family decisions. Family Meeting is a nice place to have your kids share in making routine decisions. Decide what next week's menus should be, where to go on a family outing, which TV show to watch, or how household chores should be split up. Kids will be much happier if they have a chance to give their input when decisions are made. But, give them some limits to work with. For example, if your family wants to go to a movie for your family outing this weekend, you could say, "Kids, the first thing you need to decide is what night we should go out. Then, pick a 'G' or 'PG' movie that all of us will like." This way, you let your children make decisions within limits you set. Your children may get to choose what night to go out and what movie to see, but they do not get the choice of selecting an 'R' movie. That is a limit set by you. You should always make major decisions, or decisions of a moral or legal nature.

Tips for Effective Family Meetings

Keep Family Meetings short. They should last no longer than 10-15 minutes. Keep your topics simple enough to be discussed or solved easily. As your kids improve their skills, move ahead accordingly. In the beginning, however, your goal is to keep the meeting brief.

Set a reasonable time for meetings. Make sure you choose the most opportune time for the family. Be flexible. This could mean Saturday morning or Sunday night at dinner. Some families choose to have Family Meetings after each dinner meal. Other families don't make a schedule; they have meetings whenever everyone is there. Adjust the time of your meetings to fit your needs.

Make Family Meetings fun. There will be times when you will have to make a serious decision or discuss difficult issues. These should be infrequent, however. Concentrate on sharing information or praising the good things that other family members are doing.

Use Preventive Teaching. Teach your kids how to bring up topics for discussion before the meeting takes place. Practice how to give opinions without offending someone else. Practice how to compliment others without sounding corny or insincere. And, teach your kids how to give and accept criticism without overreacting. This is a perfect time to teach your kids what to say and how to say it.

Keep a written record of decisions, schedules, issues, and so on. Use a notebook or find a convenient, well-visited spot to display them. Many parents choose to post schedules or announcements on the refrigerator. Having a visible means of recordkeeping cuts down on confusion and keeps everyone informed.

Give everyone a chance to speak. You can teach cooperation, respect, and sensitivity by assuring that everyone, from youngest to oldest, gets a voice in the way your family operates.

Give positive consequences. Give rewards and praise for listening to others, for not interrupting, for bringing up good suggestions, or for offering to help out. Family Meeting is an ideal time to praise your kids.

Use all of your teaching skills during Family Meetings. For example:

- If one of your kids receives minor criticism and begins to argue and make excuses, use Corrective Teaching.
- If your child doesn't respond to Corrective Teaching, use Teaching Self-Control.
- Use Preventive Teaching before bringing up a sensitive issue or if your child has a problem giving opinions in front of others.
- Use **SODAS** when solving problems.

Summary

Family Meetings can be one of the most important times your family spends together. You'll improve communication among family members and your kids will feel more confident about sharing opinions, accepting compliments and criticism, and making decisions.

Notes

Chapter 15

The Media – Friends or Foes?

We truly live in an information age. Kids are drenched in a media downpour of songs, TV, computer programs, movies, and magazines. Images, sounds, ideas, and sensations come rushing in at dazzling speeds. With all these messages being transmitted to our kids, most of us wonder how our children will be affected.

First of all, let's just say that the media aren't all good or all bad. There is a wonderful new world out there that our children can find – one full of excitement and discovery. There's also a negative, twisted world – one full of harmful messages they may not be equipped to handle. With this in mind, let's see what we can do as parents to gain the best of what the media have to offer and limit the negative influence they may have.

The Good News

Our children have the opportunities to be much better informed about what's going on in the world than we did when we were growing up. The "computer generation" gives them access to much more information than our outdated methods ever could. Television, through cable companies and satellite dishes, allows them to view hundreds of stations from all over the world. Our children potentially can learn so much more than we did, in much less time, and it's just at the touch of their fingertips.

The media, especially television and movies, can have a wonderful effect on children. Programs and movies that spark kids' curiosity and imagination can be fun and educational. There are programs that help them grow emotionally and learn how to appreciate and get along with others. Educational television airs many quality programs that are aimed at helping kids understand the world around them while learning more about their own potential. And some programs and movies are gentle and charming, loaded with positive messages and good fun. Watching sports gives us excitement and drama; nature shows give us a glimpse into a world we rarely see close up. We hope that television and movie executives decide to continue to provide our families with more of these healthy forms of entertainment and education.

That's the good news.

The Bad News

It's no secret that the media will do whatever it takes to survive. Their competition is fierce and they have to stay one step ahead of their rivals. Therefore, they stick with what sells. If they don't make money, they aren't going to be around very long. Products are on the market because someone buys them. They know that in advertising sex sells. They know viewers like to watch programs about bizarre lifestyles. They know people are intrigued with movies and programs whose plots revolve around drug use, violence, or "sleeping around." Beer commercials portray drinking as fun and sexy. Take a look at some of these messages peddled by many movies, music videos, magazines, and TV shows. They're not always pushing healthy values, that's for sure. Kids want to be "in," to be accepted, and to be liked by others. If they believe some of the messages from the media, they are likely to make poor choices. We know there is a lot of junk on TV and a bunch of raunchy movies and songs. And there is little doubt that kids are affected by what they see and hear.

There are hundreds of studies examining the effects of TV on kids. These studies have shown three possible negative effects of viewing television violence: Children may become less sensitive to the pain and suffering of others; they may be more fearful of the world around them; and they may be more likely to behave in aggressive or harmful ways toward others. This aggressiveness could take the form of hitting classmates, arguing, disobeying rules, and being disrespectful.

Children also can become TV "addicts." How do parents know when such a problem exists with their kids? Some warning signs that indicate that a child is watching too much television or the wrong kind of programs include: having the TV on all the time, choosing to watch TV instead of playing with friends, frequently talking about television shows or their characters and little else, "forgetting" to do homework or chores because of watching TV, or watching television just "to have something to do."

Many of the media, television included, rely on sensationalism as a "hook" to catch our attention. News programs want a "scoop." They want to gather all the dirty details of scandalous activities and they want to present it in the most dramatic way. Daytime talk shows focus on all kinds of weird lifestyles and attitudes. Most of us just scratch our heads and say, "Where do they come up with these people?" The producers of these programs seem to believe there should be a no-holds-barred approach to life and that very little should shock us anymore. We and our children are frequently bombarded with the unusual and the unconventional.

Many movies and songs also are prime examples of sensationalism. Both often contain outrageous sex and graphic violence. When kids get accustomed to continually seeing and hearing sex and violence portrayed as entertainment, they're more likely to think that's the way it is in real life. It's unhealthy for kids to buy into the message that says, "It's okay, everybody does it."

Little kids merely have to know how to operate a TV remote control or how to play a VCR tape to watch almost anything that's available. That's not very difficult for them to learn. Similarly, all they have to do is turn on a radio or push in a cassette or CD to listen to whatever music is available. There is no age requirement, no tests they have to take, no rules sent out by the media, that limit what kids can see or hear. That's a problem, and it's unfortunate because without guidance, young kids quite likely are going to sample some of the most outrageous or far-out "entertainment."

Teenagers look to the popular culture for clues about life. They find out what's in and what's not by what they see and listen to in the media. Not only do TV shows and movies give them these clues, but so do radio, rock concerts, magazines, billboards, computer networks, talk shows, CDs, and cassettes. Talk about an onslaught! The constant bombardment can be overwhelming. The media are at work, sometimes subtly, sometimes blatantly, trying to shape kids' attitudes and behaviors.

Guidelines and Suggestions for Parents

Parents are not powerless against the media's potentially harmful influences. Like the old football adage says, "The best offense is a good defense." Your defense is taking an active role in teaching your kids what's good and bad, right and wrong, about the messages they receive. The following guidelines can help you develop a plan for shielding your kids from negative media messages. Because television is especially powerful and can have the greatest impact on children, many of these tips focus on what parents can do in their home to limit its effects.

Be a good role model. Parents have a big influence on the viewing habits of their kids. If you watch a lot of TV, it's likely your children will become "couch potatoes," too. On the other hand, if you read or are involved with sports, there's a good chance your kids will read or get involved with sports. In addition to the amount of TV you watch, the type of shows you watch can influence your kids' viewing choices. If you laugh at the sexual innuendoes and profane language on a sit-com and sing the praises of that show, your seven- or eight-year-old may think that type of humor and language is acceptable, too. Take a look at the messages you are giving your kids. It might be a good idea to switch the set off more frequently or be more selective about the programs you watch. Remember that the main thing is to set a positive example.

Set a limit on the amount of time kids can watch television. Most kids will try to convince you that watching television is a right granted them by the Constitution. It isn't. Watching TV is a privilege, one that should be monitored and limited by parents.

It's your call on how much TV your kids can watch. However, most parents we talk to want some suggestions on what is healthy or "normal." Some experts recommend that daily TV viewing should be limited to one hour for preschool kids and two hours for school-age kids; viewing time can gradually increase for teenagers. Others feel that the TV should be turned off on school nights and viewing should be limited to a couple of hours on weekends. Whatever your decision, limiting the amount of time your kids can watch TV generally means that kids will put more thought into and be more selective about what they watch. This also frees up their time to get involved with other activities.

Give your kids other choices. The media has the most influence when other influences are not around. As mentioned before, it is important that families not become dependent on or preoccupied with watching television. Find some activities to take the place of TV. Sit down with your child and together come up with a list of things to do. These could include taking a bike ride, reading a book, going for a walk or run, working on a hobby, or playing a game with a brother, sister, or friend.

What about monitoring TV viewing when you're not home? That's the time to make sure your kids have some structured activity to do, like housework, yardwork, playing with the neighbor kids, or doing homework. When kids have a bundle of free time – especially unsupervised free time – it's likely they will spend it in front of the TV.

Structuring children's time lets them enjoy useful, constructive activities instead of wasting hours staring at a TV screen. Television should not be a baby-sitter. The more kids are involved in crafts, sports, exercise, reading, and other activities, the less time they have to watch television.

Make TV viewing contingent on reading and doing homework. If you are going to let your kids watch TV on school nights, have them finish their homework or chores first. In other words, "After you finish your math and science (and have your homework checked), then you can watch TV."

Evaluate what your kids are watching or listening to. You are the best judge of what is suitable for your children. Ask yourself, "Is the message given here one that I would want my kids to learn?"

Every program, movie, or song has a message or theme. Identify the main message of a particular media offering. Then ask yourself whether it will help your child grow in wisdom or understanding. If the message isn't harmful, is it in some way fun or entertaining, therefore providing healthy enjoyment for your child?

If you believe your kids are picking up language, behaviors, or attitudes from media messages that are antisocial or disrespectful, it's time to choose one (or more) of the suggestions offered here and begin to counter the media's control.

Encourage your children to choose quality programs. Look for particular programs that are designed for your child's age group. Look for shows that come highly recommended by experts. Read movie, TV, and music reviews to examine content and quality. Some television shows today carry warnings about their content. Pay attention to what those warnings say when deciding if a program is suitable for your kids.

Watch TV and movies with your kids. Watching with your kids allows you to filter through the messages your kids receive and explain controversial topics to them. Television and movies rarely depict life as it really is. This may have harmful consequences for your children. For example, on TV and in the movies, violence, sex, and drug abuse appear more often than in real life. If you are not there to explain and clarify fictional events, it's possible that your children will think they are true.

A number of studies show that if viewers do not have direct experience with what they see on TV or the big screen, they tend to believe whatever is portrayed. For example, the media can present stereotypes of various people and walks of life. Religions, races, lifestyles, cultures, ethnic backgrounds, ages – any of these can fall prey to stereotyping. Why? Because somewhere along the line, someone had success by creating negative, oversimplified images that, without proper explanation, kids may believe. That's wrong. Different just means different, not good or bad.

Watching TV with your children allows you to explain the differences between what television tells us and sells us versus what life is really like. And when your kids tell you what they got out of a program, it allows you to see how well they really understood the content. Merely explaining or pointing out fact from fiction one time is not enough. It will take many examples, many explanations, and many discussions – possibly over several years time – before they can understand television's ability to make the unreal look real.

Teach your kids how to evaluate media messages. For example, many children and teens don't really think about what they watched. It just kept them busy for awhile. You can teach them how to judge whether the messages are quality or junk, accurate or inaccurate. Talk about how the actors depicted relationships, what was good and bad about the content, and what was right and wrong with the show's messages. Show them the difference between characters who are caring and sensitive versus those who are untrustworthy or selfish. Point out the pain that violence or alcohol and drug abuse can cause. Teach them how commercials throw out images that may not be real, but are real attractive, in order to lure you into buying their products. Talk with them about the difference between aggressiveness and assertiveness. Discuss the relationships between males and females, how they should be versus how they are shown on TV and movies. Teach them that it's wrong to hit a spouse, or brother, sister, or friend.

Once again, you have an opportunity to be the primary teacher of your children – but only if you help your kids evaluate what they watch, read, and hear.

Summary

It's no secret that there are some uncreative and low-rate programs on TV. The same holds true with movies, commercials, songs, magazines, and other forms of the media. No doubt about it, there's some real garbage out there. These are the types of media offerings that parents can limit for their kids.

But there are some wonderful shows and movies, too – tasteful comedies, beautiful nature shows, interesting and stimulating documentaries, exciting sporting events, and poignant dramas. Enjoy these with your kids. Join in the fun. Make TV and movies achieve the extraordinary potential they have to be creative and educational.

Several parents in our classes were concerned that limiting television time or being more selective about what TV shows could be watched would result in an all-out rebellion by their kids. But these parents were determined to do something about their kids' viewing habits. They consistently used the Common Sense Parenting techniques they had learned to handle any problems that surfaced. When we checked with them later, they reported that they had some complaining and grumpy kids for a short while. But it wasn't very long before they reported that they were doing many more things with their kids. They played games together, shopped together, worked together, and most importantly, they talked together. The most startling news? The kids seemed happier and began to realize that they were wasting their time watching some of the shows when they could have been doing other fun things. Later, the kids mentioned that they hardly missed TV at all.

The effects of negative media messages aren't always immediately noticeable. Just because a person watches a sexual encounter in a movie or TV show doesn't mean he or she is going to run out and have sex. Just because people see violence doesn't mean they will go out and commit a violent crime. But it is clear that the more kids are bombarded with negative messages, the more likely they are to think such things are okay. Again, you are the one who can and must make a tremendous difference in teaching your kids right from wrong, what's true and what's not. Let's not leave this teaching up to the media.

Notes

Chapter 16

Social Skills

Teaching our kids what they should do is what this chapter is all about. Whereas Common Sense Parenting skills show "how" to effectively teach kids, social skills are "what" to teach kids. Social skills give parents a framework for teaching their children how to behave.

Let's define what we mean by social skills. They are sets of specific behaviors linked together in a certain order. When social skills are used correctly and at the right time, they help us get along with other people and make appropriate decisions in social situations. Think a minute about what you do when you meet someone for the first time. You probably stand up straight, look at the person, make eye contact, smile, and say your name or something like that, "It's nice to meet you." That's an example of how behaviors are strung together to make up the social skill of introducing yourself.

We use social skills everyday – greeting co-workers, asking a clerk for help, telephoning a friend, talking to a salesman about a product, giving someone a compliment – the list goes on and on. Using these skills appropriately greatly influences how other people treat us. If we have learned a wide variety of social skills, we can effectively handle more situations and get along better with more people.

Kids need to learn social skills too. They need to learn what is acceptable to other people. You can teach social skills by using Preventive Teaching or Corrective Teaching. Use Effective Praise when your kids use the skills appropriately or make an attempt to use them. In other words, you pick the teaching technique that best fits the situation you're in with your kids. The steps of each social skill neatly fit into the steps of whatever Common Sense Parenting teaching method you choose.

Using social skills appropriately increases the likelihood that your kids will know what to do or say when they deal with other people. That, in turn, means they are more likely to be successful in their interactions. You also can teach them how, why, and where they should use these skills. Parents who actively teach social skills to their children are equipping them with "survival skills" for getting along with others, for learning self-control, and generally, for having a successful life.

What Should I Teach?

Let's look at some examples of how parents can use Common Sense Parenting techniques to teach or praise social skills.

Mom asks Lalit to take out the trash and he responds with, "Why do I always have to do it?" Mom can use Corrective Teaching to teach the social skill of following instructions.

Mallika and her Dad are sitting at the dinner table when she begins telling him about a friend who was drinking beer at last night's football game. Dad can use Effective Praise to point out the social skill of telling the truth.

Dad is in the kitchen when Venkat rushes in and says he's going to a friend's house. Dad says that dinner is almost ready so he needs to stay home. Venkat begins complaining. Dad can use Corrective Teaching to teach the social skill of accepting "No" answers.

Rajni has had a problem understanding her math homework in the past. Before she begins her homework, her mom reminds her how to ask for help with problems she doesn't understand. Mom used Preventive Teaching to encourage Rajni to use the social skill of asking for help.

In each of these examples, the parents taught a specific social skill that will help their kids in future situations.

Later in this chapter, a more detailed explanation of 16 important social skills is presented. The helpful hints that accompany the social skills are examples of what you can say to your children as you teach these skills. The behaviors listed for each of the skills are general guidelines; they can be changed according to what you feel your kids need to learn.

These 16 skills can be used many times each day to help kids do well at home and in school. More importantly, mastering these skills will be the key to helping your kids achieve success and avoid conflicts with others.

Kids learn at different rates so you will need to alter your teaching accordingly. Some kids catch on right away; others require more practice and repetition in order to really learn what you're teaching. Some children don't have the attention span for a lengthy teaching session. Feel free to adjust and modify the steps of the social skills based on your child's ability.

Using Preventive Teaching to Teach Social Skills

Let's look at an example of a mother using Preventive Teaching to teach her eight-year-old how to accept a "No" answer. In the past, when her son was told "No," he would frequently argue, whine, or pout. These behaviors have caused problems not only at home, but in school as well.

The steps she wants to teach in accepting "No" are:

1. Look at the person.
2. Say "Okay."
3. Calmly ask for a reason if you really don't understand.
4. If you disagree, bring it up later.

Here's how Preventive Teaching works in this situation.

Mom – "Jitendra, because school is starting soon, I'd like to talk with you about a few things."
Jitendra - "Okay."
Mom – "You know, sometimes you're going to want to do something and your teacher might say 'No.'"
Jitendra – "Yeah, that's happened before. Especially with Mrs. Bias."

Describe what you would like

Mom – "That's exactly right, Jitendra. So I want to practice with you how to accept a 'No' answer. Let's pretend Mrs. Bias just told you 'No.' The first thing you need to do is look at her. Don't look away or look down. Okay?"

Jitendra – "Uh huh."

Mom – "After you look at her, then you need to say 'Okay' in a nice voice." Jitendra - "Okay."

Mom – "Good. If you really don't understand why you were told 'No,' then calmly ask for a reason. But only if you don't understand. Okay?"

Jitendra – "Yeah. I understand."

Mom – "Great. If you disagree with the answer your teacher gave, make sure you bring it up later."

Give a reason

Mom – "If you learn how to accept a 'No' answer and not argue, then your teacher is more likely to listen to what you have to say."

Jitendra – "Yeah, I see what you mean."

Mom – "Good. Now, remember to look at the teacher, say 'Okay,' calmly ask for a reason if you don't understand, and if you disagree, bring it up later. Got it?"

Jitendra - "Yes, I do."

Practice

Mom – "Okay, let's pretend that I'm Mrs. Bias and you're going to ask me to play the computer...."

Mom and Jitendra would then practice various situations he might face during school. As Jitendra practices, Mom can see where he does well and where he struggles. For example, maybe his voice tone sounds rather harsh or negative or he fidgets when he talks. Mom can practice with Jitendra until he feels more comfortable with each step of the skill. She also can supply real-life reasons why learning this social skill will make things go smoother for him.

Notice that Mom picked a time to use Preventive Teaching when Jitendra was cooperative and wasn't busy doing something else. She also used a calm, conversational tone.

Also, notice how Mom continued to ask if Jitendra understood. Always make the steps of the skill easy to understand and within your child's ability level. If your children are younger or have a hard time remembering each step, you could teach and practice the first two steps until your kids understand them completely, then later add the other two.

Using Corrective Teaching to Teach Social Skills

In other situations, you may find that Corrective Teaching is needed to teach social skills. For example, let's say that Dad heard 10-year-old Bharati call her sister names like "stupid"and "idiot." Here's an example of how Corrective Teaching can be used to teach the skill of asking for help.

Stop the problem behavior
Dad – "Bharati, when I walked into the room, I heard you call Tulika names like 'stupid' and 'idiot.' I'm sure that hurt her feelings, don't you think?"
Bharati – (whining) "But Dad, she was bugging me."
Dad – "That may be true, but calling her names isn't the way to take care of it."

Give a consequence
Dad – "For calling Tulika names, I want you to apologize to her and then help her clean up the toys in her bedroom."
Bharati – "Oh,, all right."

Describe what you want

Dad – "When Tulika is bugging you, decide exactly what it is that bothers you. Then ask her to stop. If she continues to do things that bug you, come to mom or me and ask for help in solving the problem. Okay?"

Practice what you want

Dad – "Before you apologize, show me how you would ask me for help if Tulika is bugging you."
Bharati – "Okay. I should say something to you like, 'Daddy, Tulika keeps grabbing my toys and sticking her tongue out at me. I asked her to stop but she wouldn't. Can you help me out?'"

Summary

Teaching your kids social skills can help them build strong relationships with others. When teaching these skills, use simple explanations and examples. Use Effective Praise when you see them using a skill appropriately.

Teach each of the skills step by step. Take time to explain to your children when they can use these skills and why these skills will help them. Let them see how one skill overlaps into other areas. For example, knowing how to accept criticism from a teacher is very similar to accepting criticism from any adult authority figure. Learning how to ask for help from a store clerk is similar to asking a police officer for directions.

Make learning social skills fun. Praise your kids or reward them with something special for taking the time to learn. They might not realize the benefits of learning social skills right away. But the more they use these skills and see the positive way other people respond to them, the more the skills will "sink in."

Finally, be patient. After your kids learn a new skill, it may take awhile before they are comfortable using it – before it really becomes a part of them. Learning new skills is an ongoing process. It's not a "done deal" just because skills have been practiced once or twice. Comparisons can be drawn to almost any other skill we learn. You don't learn how to dribble a basketball in one try; you don't learn how to drive a car the first time you climb behind the wheel. We don't become good at anything without practice, practice, practice.

Social skills give your kids a solid foundation for getting along with others and being more successful in many areas of their lives. Kids of all ages can benefit. Small children can learn to follow instructions and give compliments just as easily as teenagers can. Don't hesitate to teach your kids acceptable ways to behave. The time to begin teaching social skills is now.

Following Instructions

When you are given an instruction, you should:

1. **Look at the person who is talking.**
2. **Show that you understand** ("I understand," "Okay,"or "I'll do it"). Make sure you wait until the person is done talking before you do what is asked. It is usually best to answer, but sometimes nodding your head will be enough to show the person that you understand.
3. **Do what is asked in the best way that you can.**
4. **Let the person know that you have finished.**

It is important to do what is asked because it shows your ability to cooperate and it saves time. Following instructions will help you in school, at home, with adults and friends.

Helpful Hints:

- After finding out exactly what has been asked, start the task immediately.
- If you have any doubts that doing what is asked will result in some type of negative consequence for you, or you don't understand, ask a trusted adult.
- Do what is asked as pleasantly as possible.
- Check back as soon as you finish. This increases the chance that you will get credit for doing a job well. It also means that somebody else won't have time to mess it up before you check back.

Accepting Criticism

When others tell you how they think you can improve, they give you criticism. When you accept criticism:

1. **Look at the person**. Don't give negative facial expressions.
2. **Stay calm and quiet while the person is talking.**
3. **Show you understand** ("Okay" or "I understand").
4. **Try to correct the problem**. If you are asked to do something different, do it. If you are asked to stop doing something, stop it. If you can't give a positive response, at least give one that will not get you into trouble ("Okay," "I understand," or "Thanks").

Being able to accept criticism shows maturity and prevents having problems with people in authority. If you can control yourself and listen to what others have to say about how you can improve, it will result in fewer problems for you. And, the criticism may really help you!

Helpful Hints:

- It is most important that you stay calm. Take a deep breath if necessary.
- Criticizing, becoming angry, or making negative facial expressions will only get you into more trouble.
- When you respond to the person who is giving you criticism, use as pleasant a voice tone as possible. You will receive criticism for the rest of your life – all people do. The way you handle it determines how you are treated by others.
- Most criticism is designed to help you; however, sometimes it is hard to accept. If you don't agree with the criticism, ask me or another trusted adult.
- Always ask questions if you don't understand. (But don't play games by asking questions when you do understand and are just being stubborn.) Give yourself a chance to improve!

Accepting 'No' Answers

1. **Look at the person.**
2. **Say "Okay."**
3. **Calmly ask for a reason if you really don't understand.**
4. **If you disagree, bring it up later.**

You will be told "No" many times in your life. Getting angry and upset only leads to more problems. If you are able to appropriately accept the "No" answer, people will view you as cooperative and mature.

Helpful Hints:

- Don't stare, make faces, or look away. If you are upset, control your emotions. Try to relax and stay calm. Listening carefully will help you understand what the other person is saying.
- Answer right away and speak clearly. Take a deep breath if you feel upset.
- Don't ask for a reason every time or you will be viewed as a complainer. People will think you are serious about wanting to know a reason if you ask for one calmly. Don't keep asking for reasons after you receive one. Use what you learn in these situations in the future.
- Take some time to plan how you are going to approach the person who told you "No." Plan in advance what you are going to say. Accept the answer, even if it is still "No." Be sure to thank the person for listening. At least you had the opportunity to share your opinion.

Staying Calm

When people feel angry or upset, it's hard to stay calm. When we feel like "blowing up," we sometimes make poor choices. And usually when we make poor choices, we regret it later. If you feel that you are going to lose self-control, you should:

1. **Take a deep breath.**
2. **Relax your muscles.**
3. **Tell yourself to "Be calm," or count to ten.**
4. **Share your feelings.** After you are relaxed, tell someone you trust what is bothering you.
5. **Try to solve the situation that made you upset.**

It is important to stay calm since worse things always seem to happen if you lose your temper. If you can stay calm, other people will depend on you more often. They will see you as mature and able to handle even the worst situations. Teachers and employers will respect you and see you as someone who can keep "cool."

Helpful Hints:

- You might try to talk yourself into the idea that "blowing up" is the only thing to do, or that the other person or thing "deserves it." Forget it. It doesn't work that way. And, you're setting yourself up to get more or worse consequences. Be calm.
- After you have calmed down, pat yourself on the back. Even adults have a hard time with self-control. If you can control yourself, you will have accomplished something that many adults are still struggling with. Give yourself some praise! You have done the right thing.

Disagreeing With Others

When you don't agree with another person's opinion or decision, you should:

1. **Remain calm**. Getting upset will only make matters worse.
2. **Look at the person**. This shows that you have confidence.
3. **Begin with a positive or neutral statement**. "I know you are trying to be fair but...."
4. **Explain why you disagree with the decision**. Keep your voice tone level and controlled. Be brief and clear.
5. **Listen as the other person explains his or her side of the story**.
6. **Calmly accept whatever decision is made**.
7. **Thank the person for listening, regardless of the outcome**.

It is important to disagree in a calm manner because it increases the chances that the other person will listen. This may be the only opportunity you have to get the decision changed. You have a right to be able to express your opinions. But, you lose that right if you become upset or aggressive. If the other person feels that you are going to lose self-control, you stand very little chance of getting your views across.

Helpful Hints:

- You're not going to win every time. Some decisions will not change. However, learning how to disagree calmly may help change some of them.
- Don't try to change everything. People will view you as a pest.
- If you are calm and specific when you disagree, people will respect you for the mature way you handle situations. It pays off in the long run!

Asking For Help

When you need help with something, you should:

1. **Decide what the problem is.**
2. **Ask to speak to the person most likely to help you.**
3. **Look at the person, clearly describe what you need help with, and ask the person in a pleasant voice tone.**
4. **Thank the person for helping you.**

It is important to ask others for help because it is the best way to solve problems you can't figure out. Asking for help in a pleasant manner makes it more likely that someone will help you.

Helpful Hints:

- It is nice to figure things out by yourself. Sometimes, this isn't possible. Asking someone who has more experience, or has had more success with a similar problem, is a way to learn how to solve the problem the next time.
- Sometimes, people become frustrated when they can't figure something out. Sometimes, they even become mad. Learn to ask for help before you get to this point and you will have more successes than failures.
- Always tell the person who is helping you how much you appreciate the help. It might be nice to offer your help the next time that person needs something.

Asking Permission

When you need to get permission from someone else, you should:

1. **Look at the other person**.
2. **Be specific when you ask permission**. The other person should know exactly what you are requesting.
3. **Be sure to ask rather than demand**. "May I please...?"
4. **Give reasons if necessary**.
5. **Accept the decision**.

It is important to ask permission whenever you want to do something or use something that another person is responsible for. Asking permission shows your respect for others and increases the chances that your request will be granted.

Helpful Hints:

- It is always wise to ask permission to use something that doesn't belong to you. It doesn't matter if it is a sack of potato chips or someone's bike – ask permission!
- Sometimes you won't get what you want. But if you have asked permission politely and correctly, it is more likely that you may get what you want the next time.
- It may help you to think about how you would feel if someone used something of yours without asking first. Besides feeling like that person was not polite and did not respect your property, you would be worried that the item could get broken or lost.

Getting Along With Others

To be successful in dealing with people, you should:

1. **Listen to what is being said when another person talks to you.**
2. **Say something positive if you agree with what that person said.** If you don't agree, say something that won't cause an argument. Use a calm voice tone.
3. **Show interest in what the other person has to say.** Try to understand his or her point of view.

It is important to get along with others because you will be working and dealing with other people most of your life. If you can get along with others, it is more likely that you will be successful in whatever you do. Getting along shows sensitivity and respect, and makes it more likely that other people will behave the same way. In other words, treat others the way you want to be treated!

Helpful Hints:

- Sometimes it is not easy to get along with others. If someone does something that you do not like, or says something negative, you may feel like behaving the same way, but don't. Stop yourself from saying things that can hurt others' feelings. Teasing, cussing, and insults will only make matters worse. It is better to ignore others' negative behavior than to act like them.
- Getting along with others takes some effort. It is hard to understand why some people act the way they do. Try to put yourself in their place and maybe it will be easier to understand.
- If you find that you don't like someone's behavior, it is better to say nothing rather than something negative.

Apologizing

When you have done something that hurts another person's feelings or results in negative consequences for another person, you should apologize.

1. **Look at the person**. It shows confidence.
2. **Say what you are sorry about**. "I'm sorry I said that" or "I'm sorry, I didn't listen to what you said."
3. **Make a follow-up statement if the person says something to you**. "Is there any way I can make it up to you?" or "It won't happen again."
4. **Thank the person for listening** (even if the person did not accept your apology).

It is important to apologize because it shows that you are sensitive to others' feelings. It increases the chances that other people will be sensitive to your feelings in return. Apologizing also shows that you are responsible enough to admit mistakes.

Helpful Hints:

- It is easy to avoid making apologies; it takes guts to be mature enough to do it. Convince yourself that making an apology is the best thing to do and then do it!
- If the other person is upset with you, the response you receive may not be real nice at that time. Be prepared to take whatever the other person says. Be confident that you are doing the right thing.
- When people look back on your apology, they will see that you were able to realize what you did wrong. They will think more positively of you in the future.
- An apology won't erase what you did wrong. But, it may help change a person's opinion of you in the long run.

Conversation Skills

When you are talking with someone, you should:

1. **Look at the other person.**
2. **Answer any questions asked of you, and give complete answers.** Just saying "Yes" or "No," does not give the other person any information that can keep the conversation going.
3. **Avoid negative statements.** Talking about past trouble you were in, bragging, name-calling, cussing, or making other negative statements gives a bad impression.
4. **Use appropriate grammar.** Slang can be used with friends, but don't use it when guests are present.
5. **Start or add to conversation by asking questions, talking about new or exciting events, or asking the other person what he or she thinks about something.**

It is important to have good conversation skills because you can tell others what you think about something and get their opinions. Good conversation skills make guests feel more comfortable and visits with you more enjoyable. Conversation skills also help you when you apply for a job or meet new people.

Helpful Hints:

- Always include the other person's ideas in the conversation. If you don't, it won't be a conversation!
- Smile and show interest in what the other person has to say, even if you don't agree with the person.
- Keep up on current events so that you have a wide range of things to talk about. People who can talk about what's happening and are good at conversation are usually well-liked and admired by other people.

Giving Compliments

When you say something nice about someone, you should:

1. **Look at the other person.**
2. **Give the compliment.** Tell him or her exactly what you liked.
3. **Make a follow-up statement.** If the person says "Thanks," say "You're welcome," in return.

Giving compliments shows that you can notice the accomplishments of others. It shows friendliness; people like being around someone who is pleasant and can say nice things. It also shows that you have confidence in your ability to talk to others.

Helpful Hints:

- Think of the exact words you want to use before you give the compliment. It will make you feel more confident and less likely to fumble around for words.
- Mean what you say. People can tell the difference between real and phony.
- Don't overdo it. A couple of sentences will do – "You did a good job at..." or "You really did well in...."
- It is nice to smile and be enthusiastic when you give compliments. It makes the other person feel that you really mean it.

Accepting Compliments

Whenever someone says something nice to you, you should:

1. **Look at the other person.**
2. **Listen to what the other person is saying.**
3. **Don't interrupt.**
4. **Say "Thanks," or something that shows you appreciate what was said.**

Being able to accept compliments shows that you can politely receive another person's opinion about something you have done. It also increases the chance that you will receive future compliments.

Helpful Hints:

- Many times it is easy to feel uncomfortable when you receive a compliment. For example, when someone gives you a compliment on a sweater you are wearing, and you say, "Whattya mean, this old rag?" Statements like that make the other person less likely to give you compliments in the future. Don't reject what the other person is saying.
- People give compliments for a variety of reasons. Don't waste a lot of time wondering why someone gave you a compliment. Just appreciate the fact that someone took the time to say something nice to you!

Listening To Others

When someone is speaking, you should:

1. **Look at the person who is talking.**
2. **Sit or stand quietly.**
3. **Wait until the person is through talking.** Don't interrupt; it will seem like you are complaining.
4. **Show that you understand.** Say, "Okay," "Thanks," "I see," etc., or ask the person to explain if you don't understand.

It is important to listen because it shows pleasantness and cooperation. It increases the chances that people will listen to you. And, it increases the chances that you will do the correct thing since you understand.

Helpful Hints:

- If you are having trouble listening, think of how you would feel if other people didn't listen to you.
- Try to remember everything the person said. Write it down if you feel you may forget.
- People who learn to listen well do better on jobs and in school.
- Don't show any negative facial expressions. Continue looking at the other person, and nod your head or occasionally say something to let the other person know you are still listening.

Telling the Truth

When you have done something, whether it's good or bad, you need to tell the truth. Telling the truth makes other people trust you. If they can believe what you say, you will be trusted. Sometimes, people will ask you questions about your involvement in a situation. To tell the truth you should:

1. **Look at the person.**
2. **Say exactly what happened if asked to supply information.**
3. **Answer any other questions.** This can be what you did or did not do, or what someone else did or did not do.
4. **Don't leave out important facts.**
5. **Admit to mistakes or errors if you made them.**

It is important to tell the truth because people are more likely to give you a second chance if they have been able to trust you in the past. We all make mistakes, but lying will lead to more problems. If you get the reputation of being a liar, it is hard for people to believe what you say. Plus, when you tell the truth, you should feel confident that you have done the right thing.

Helpful Hints:

- Telling the truth is hard. Many times, it will seem that lying is the easiest way out of a situation. When people find out that you have lied, the consequences are much worse.
- Lying is the opposite of telling the truth. Lying is similar to stealing or cheating. All will result in negative consequences for you.

Introducing Yourself

When you introduce yourself, you should:

1. **Stand up straight**. If you are sitting or doing something else, stop immediately and greet the person.
2. **Look at the other person**.
3. **After saying namaste, say your name clearly and loudly enough to be heard easily.** This shows the other person that you are confident.
4. **Make a friendly statement**. ("Nice to meet you.")

It is important to introduce yourself because it shows your ability to meet new people confidently. It makes others feel more comfortable and you make a good first impression. Being able to introduce yourself will be helpful on job interviews and is a pleasant way to "break the ice."

Helpful Hints:

- Being pleasant is very important when introducing yourself. If you are gruff or your voice is harsh, people won't get a good impression of you. Smile when giving your name to the other person.
- Introductions are the first step in conversation. If you start out on the right foot, it is more likely that you will have a pleasant conversation. Make your first impression a good impression.
- If the other person does not give his or her name, say "And your name is?"
- When you meet a person again, you will have to choose how to re- introduce yourself. If there is a long time in between, or if the person may have forgotten who you are, then you should follow the same steps as above. If the time in between is short, you may choose just to say, "Hi, in case you forgot, I'm...."
- Try to remember the other person's name. Other people will be impressed when you take time to remember them.

Showing Sensitivity To Others

1. **Express interest and concern for others, especially when they are having troubles.**
2. **Recognize that disabled people deserve the same respect as anyone else.**
3. **Apologize or make amends for hurting someone's feelings or causing harm.**
4. **Recognize that people of different races, religions, and backgrounds deserve to be treated the same way as you would expect to be treated.**

If you help others, they are more likely to help you. And saying you're sorry shows that you can take responsibility for your actions and can admit when you've done something wrong. A disability does not make a person inferior. Helping people with disabilities and treating everyone equally shows that you believe that although people are different, they all deserve respect.

Helpful Hints:

- If you see someone in trouble, ask if you can help.
- Sometimes, just showing you care is enough to help a person get through a difficult time.
- Be ready to help a disabled person when necessary by doing such things as holding open a door, carrying a package, or giving up your seat.
- Don't stare at disabled people or make comments about their special needs.
- You can harm someone by what you fail to do, just as easily as by what you do. Some examples are breaking a promise or not sticking up for someone who is being picked on. If you hurt someone, apologize immediately and sincerely.
- Don't make jokes or rude comments about the color of someone's skin or what he or she believes.

Notes

Chapter 17

Peer Pressure

"Come on. No one will find out. I promise."
"Let's go. Everyone's going to be there. It'll be a blast."
"Let's ditch school. The guys are gettin' together downtown."
"Just this once. Trust me."

Peer pressure. The very words make most parents cringe. The influence of friends is a powerful force in almost everyone's life. Kids face this pressure from the first time they play with other children. And with all of the things available to kids today, peer pressure is a major worry for parents with teenagers. You can't make peer pressure go away; it is a natural part of growing up. But you can help your child learn how to deal with it.

First of all, having friends and making independent decisions are part of normal development for children. Although the term "peer pressure" usually conjures up negative images, your children's friends can be very positive influences in the lives of your children. Friends can encourage one another to do good things, to try harder in extracurricular activities or schoolwork, and to avoid other kids who might not have their best interests at heart. In this way, peer pressure is very healthy.

However, when most parents think of peer pressure, they don't always think about those healthy images. They know kids can be very persuasive with other kids. Teenagers especially face many situations that could lead to big trouble. The availability of drugs and alcohol and the lure of gangs and permissive sex are just some of the major concerns parents have today. We certainly aren't downplaying these influences, but it is important for parents to realize that there are ways to counter the impact of peer pressure.

The following tips may help your kids avoid or deal with the negative influences of their peer group.

Spend Time Together

Recent studies indicate that children who feel close to their parents are less likely to be negatively influenced by other kids than children who don't have good relationships with their parents. Children who have strong relationships with their parents also are more likely to be confident in their abilities and able to solve problems on their own. No one can build a strong relationship or gain trust and respect from other people overnight. All of the teaching you do – not just one or two interactions – strengthens and enhances your relationships with your children. Many parents don't realize the powerful influence they have on their children. All of the love and concern, all of the time you spend with your children, greatly affects the types of decisions they make.

Many children live in a household where both parents work. Many others live in a single-parent household. Some parents find it hard to hold down a job, maintain a home, pay bills, and be with their children. There is a strict demand on time. Regardless of how much time we'd like to spend with our kids, life's obligations and obstacles sometimes trip us up. The only way to assure that you will have time with your kids is to make time. Make it a priority. Schedule time if necessary. But it is vital that you spend time with your kids. It's not something you can put off until tomorrow. Any parent with grown children can tell you how fast time flies, and before you know it, your kids will be on their own, too.

As children get older, they become more involved with outside activities and friends. They slip farther and farther away from their parents' guidance. This is not a cause for alarm; it is the normal progression from childhood to adulthood – becoming independent by learning who they are and what they believe in. How well children respond to the rest of the world as they grow up depends a great deal on the quality of their relationships with their parents. If you are the parent of an older child who always seems to be busy and is never around you, find something that he or she enjoys and do it together. Go fishing, shopping, out to a movie, on a walk, out to eat; it doesn't matter what you do as much as the fact that you spend time with one another. The more you are around your kids, the more likely they are to tell you about what's happening in their lives, and the more guidance you can give them for battling negative peer pressure.

Use Preventive Teaching and SODAS

Some of the time you spend with your kids should be used to discuss problems and concerns they might face. This gives you an opportunity to offer advice and reinforce your family's morals and values – the very essence of what you believe in. Your children's standards of acceptable behavior are developed from what you teach and what you say and do.

Because you know your children's good and bad qualities, their tendencies, and their likes and dislikes, Preventive Teaching can be used to prepare them for times when they have to make difficult choices. Teach them how to say "No" and mean it. Teach them how to appropriately disagree, share their opinions, and help friends who are in need. These skills are powerful when your children use them confidently and consistently. They can help your kids avoid negative influences from their friends and other youth.

Help your kids come up with short statements – one-liners to use in given situations. For example, if your teenage daughter is being pressured to skip school, she can say, "I can't. I want to keep my grades up," or "I'm behind in science class already and I can't get further behind." If all else fails, you can be the perfect reason. Your child can say, "My parents will ground me for a month," or "My parents would freak and I wouldn't be able to go out this weekend." The important thing is to let your kids know that they have lots of ways to say "No" if they take the time to think ahead.

As we mention throughout this book, practicing a skill is crucial to feeling comfortable when using it in a real-life situation. If problems with peers continue, use the SODAS method to find workable solutions.

Kids should have a variety of options and solutions for the problems they face with peers. There is no perfect solution that can be used in every situation. There are too many things that could foil their plans. And just because you and your children practiced how to say "No," it doesn't mean that their friends will accept it right away. Their friends can be very persistent. They can nag and badger or be coy and convincing until your kids feel like giving in. So, you have to teach your kids to stay calm and confident, and to be just as persistent with their answers. This also might be a good time to talk with your children about whether kids who don't respect their decisions are true friends.

As your children get older, they will find dangers lurking around every corner. Don't let them be caught unaware. The evils of drugs, drinking, gangs, sex, and other illegal or immoral activities are prevalent in today's culture; there's no denying their impact on our society. Your kids will feel the pressure from their peers to get involved. Therefore, you must teach your kids how to deal with them, avoid them, or cast them aside. It's not an easy task for young people. They want to be liked so the temptation to go along with the crowd is always there. Give them the benefit of your experience and knowledge by using Preventive Teaching and SODAS.

Listen to Your Children

Listen carefully to what your children say. Talk with them instead of at them. For example, bedtime is a good time to recap your children's day and talk with them about what's going on in their lives. Dinnertime also lets family members share information with one another. And for the many families that always seem to be on the run taking kids to sports and other activities, time spent riding in the car is ideal for having family chats.

How you talk to your kids is important, too. Get at eye level and eliminate distractions. Ask questions, but don't interrogate. Keep it brief; don't lecture. Help your kids feel comfortable when they tell you things. If they fear your reaction, they won't volunteer much information.

Some parents make the mistake of rushing in and flooding their children with advice when their kids tell them about a problem. Even when your children tell you something that distresses you, try to remain calm and hear them out. Keep your cool, especially when they tell you things that go against your beliefs or that honestly frighten you. You cannot help them come up with solutions to their problems if you don't know the whole story. Remember, their "kid" world is sometimes completely different from our "adult" world. They don't have the experience needed to make some decisions. There are many new experiences waiting and they need time to talk and discover how to handle these situations.

There will be times when your kids are purposely vague about a problem they're having with friends or classmates. They don't want to be tattletales and they may be worried that they will lose their friends if they tell you about them. They also may worry about your reaction. At the same time, they may be confused and, deep down inside, really want your help. That's why making them feel comfortable about telling you things is very important. By listening calmly, asking brief clarifying questions, and saying understanding words, you will help your children "open up" when they are having problems.

It's also extremely important to praise your kids when they do share their thoughts and opinions with you, stand up to negative influences, report a concern, or tell you about a problem. Reinforce their decisions; let them know they did the right thing. If things didn't work out as well as expected, praise their courage for trying. A few words of support can go a long way toward helping them make, and be confident in their abilities to arrive at good decisions in the future. For example, you can simply say, "Thanks for telling me that. It took a lot of courage," or "You should be proud of yourself for standing up to those guys," or "I know that it was hard for you to tell me, but now that we know what the problem is, we can deal with it together."

Monitor

Monitoring what your children do also helps them avoid peer pressure. By monitoring, we mean keeping track of and watching over your kids, and having them check in and report where they are, who they're with, and what they're doing. We don't mean hovering over them and watching their every move, or conducting some kind of undercover surveillance on them. That is an overprotective, almost smothering, behavior, rather than one that allows them to act independently, yet with your guidance and support.

We worked with one parent who had four teenagers. She posted this note in a highly visible place on the refrigerator (a spot she knew her kids would visit often): "Before you ask me to go anywhere, be prepared to tell me where you are going, how you'll get there and back, when you'll be home, what you'll be doing, and who you'll be with." This parent had a pretty good idea of what her kids were doing when they weren't at home. She also consistently delivered consequences for their behavior – positive for following through on their plans, negative for not doing what they said they were going to do. This was one way she helped monitor her kids and keep track of what they were doing.

Regardless of whether your children are young or old, monitoring their activities keeps you involved and lets your kids know that you care about them and their safety. An additional benefit is that your kids will have fewer opportunities to get into trouble because they aren't spending too much unsupervised time with other kids. Let's put it this way: If you don't monitor your kids, someone else will be in charge of what they do and what they learn. That's taking a big chance.

Checking on your kids is one way you can help them avoid peer pressure. You can alert them to pitfalls, teach and discipline, and help them solve problems on their own. Monitoring also gives you many more opportunities to "catch 'em being good," which leads to more times you can use Effective Praise. So don't be afraid to set some guidelines and check up on your kids.

Summary

Peers will always have an influence on your children – sometimes good, sometimes bad. But don't fail to recognize how much influence you have. You can help your kids learn to recognize the wrong kind of peer pressure and teach them what to do about it. Even if you feel your children have already been negatively influenced by peer pressure, it's not too late to start making changes for the better.

Notes

Chapter 18

Helping Children Succeed in School

Some students breeze through school. They find classes interesting, challenging, and stimulating. They like to read independently and are often found scouring the shelves of libraries for new and exciting things to learn. They come home from school each day and sit down to do their homework without being asked. If they come across a word they don't understand, they find a dictionary and look up the word. If your child is one of these students, you can probably skip this chapter. On the other hand, if your child

- has difficulty getting homework done without being asked several times, or
- loses assignments between home and school, or
- postpones schoolwork until the last minute, or
- prefers to skip rather than attend classes, or
- has any number of other school-related problems,

then you may find the information in this chapter helpful.

Many of the problems that kids experience at school are related to their behavior rather than their academic abilities. For example, many children who do poorly in a course often don't do homework, prepare for tests, or attend class regularly. They may be disruptive in class, thereby missing much of the information that the other students are learning. Some of the most successful students are the ones who also behave well in class. They follow instructions, accept criticism, and get along with their classmates. Students who have positive social skills have a better chance of doing well academically.

There are several things that parents can do at home that can improve their children's school behavior and academic performance. The first thing you can do is make sure that your child can (and will) follow instructions. Following instructions is the first step toward getting your kids to succeed in school, at home, or in society in general.

Get involved in your children's education. Studies have shown that parental involvement in school is closely tied to children's success in school. Involvement with your children's school should occur daily. Asking your kids about their school day is a good place to start.

You may be thinking, "Hey wait a minute! I've tried to ask my kids about their school day and I don't get a lot of information!" Getting kids to share information about their school day can be a challenge. Here's a typical example of one of those exchanges.

Mom – "How was school today?"

Son – "All right."

Mom – "What did you do?"

Son – "Not much."

And the conversation goes on like this for another 30 seconds before mom gives up hope of getting more than one-word answers or guttural responses from her son.

The type of questions that have a greater chance of paying off with more of a response are ones that request action. Ask your child to actually show or tell you something specific, rather than asking a question that will result in a quick response. For example, requests like, "Show me what you did in school today," or "Tell me about your math class today," are more likely to get a substantial response than asking, "How was school today?" Additionally, asking questions about certain aspects of school that you know your children enjoy can open the door to talking about other school topics. For example, ask them for an update on classmates or friends. Ask them which teachers or classes they like best or dislike most.

School involvement also can include these activities:

Setting up time for homework

Helping with homework

Contacting teachers
Using school notes
Working with teachers to solve school problems

Setting up time for homework. Studies have shown, and common sense supports, that studying at home can help improve children's performance in school. Here are a few hints for helping kids get their homework completed on a regular basis.

- Establish one central location for completing homework. Make sure the place has a clean working surface (a kitchen table or a desk in your child's room).
- Keep the area as quiet as possible for study time. It's not likely that you can shut out all background noise, but shut off the TV and radio, and try to get rid of any other distraction, such as the telephone. If you have younger children, keep them occupied by reading them a story or having them play outside while their older sister or brother is studying.
- Set a specific amount of study time for each school night (typically, Sunday through Thursday nights). For children in the elementary grades, study time might typically last 30 to 45 minutes; for junior high students, 45 to 75 minutes; and for high school students, 60 to 90 minutes or more is recommended. The amount of time can be increased if the child needs more time to complete assignments.
- With children who have difficulty concentrating for long periods of time, divide their study time into smaller periods. For example, some children, especially younger ones, may do better studying for 15 minutes, taking a short break, then studying for another 15 minutes. If they know they'll get a break, then they may be more likely to concentrate during the actual study time.

- Schedule the study time so that it best fits your and your children's routines. For some children, right after school is a good time for homework. However, for parents who work outside of the home, it is often tough to monitor and help with homework right after school. So, early evening, at a time that doesn't conflict with their favorite TV show or after-school activities, may work best for these families. Picking a time when there are few interruptions and when children are most likely to concentrate increases the probability that homework will get completed.
- Remember "Grandma's rule" when setting up study time "First, eat your vegetables, then you can have your dessert." Homework is much more likely to get done if you have study time before allowing your children to watch TV, talk on the phone, or go to a friend's house.
- If children do not bring assignments home, or they tell you they completed all their homework in school, they can always do projects for extra credit, or read books, magazines, or newspapers. The goal is to have them learning. If the first step toward establishing a life-long habit of reading for a child comes from reading a sports magazine, then start there. In time, he or she may be willing to read more difficult books.

Here are some additional activities for children who say they have no homework to do during study time.

- Have them read aloud to a younger brother or sister.
- Read a newspaper article about world events, nutrition, teenage problems, or any other interesting topic.
- Write letters to grandparents, friends, or relatives.
- Read a book.
- Cut coupons and add up the amount of money saved.

- Help their brother or sister with homework or tutor a friend or neighbor.
- Write in a journal or diary.
- Make a list of the things they want to do for the week.

The number of constructive activities your children can do during study time is endless. Learning can be fun, both at home and at school. This is where you get the opportunity to make it fun at home.

Helping with homework. Given the schedules of most parents, finding time to help children with homework is no easy feat. Nevertheless, the time you can spend together keeps you involved with your child, decreases the chances that your child will fall behind in class, and shows your child that you value education.

Okay, so maybe you don't feel comfortable helping with fractions, physics, or diagramming sentences. There are still some things you can do to help your children complete their assignments. First, be available and watch for opportunities to praise them for staying on task with their homework.

Second, set a positive example. Read a book, write a letter, balance the checkbook, or make a grocery list while they are studying. Leave the TV and radio off. (If need be, videotape your favorite show and watch it later.) You help set the tone for the importance of homework. When there are questions you can't answer, and there will be, your children can call a classmate or teacher. Then, have them explain the answer to you so you both can understand what they're doing.

Third, help your children organize their time and materials (for example, pens and paper) for homework. This might involve having them use a notebook for keeping track of their assignments. This notebook can be their school planner. At the end of each class, they write the assignment in their planner and bring it and related school books home after school. You also can use the planner to start discussions about their school day.

Finally, they need to get started studying at the designated time. Kids generally do better if they have a routine to follow. Pick a time that works best for both you and your kids. There will be times when activities prevent your kids from studying at that time, but those activities should be the exception rather than the rule.

Contacting teachers. Contact between parents and teachers can be a problem. To be frank, teachers often blame students' problems on parents and parents often blame children's school problems on teachers. Instead of assigning blame, work together to help your children get the best education possible.

Start by attending the open-house that almost every school offers at the beginning of the school year. Introduce yourself and be sure to mention to the teachers that they can call you whenever necessary. Explain that you are interested in keeping informed about your child's progress and that you may call during their free period if that's acceptable to them. Then, at the end of the first week or so, call the teacher and ask how your child is doing in school. You also can share with the teacher some of the skills you are teaching your child, such as following instructions and asking for help. Discuss how the teacher might be able to help by focusing on similar skills at school. Keep the teacher informed about major events in your child's life, such as the death of a relative or other emotional situations. Always thank the teachers for the work they do and the time they take with your child.

Parents typically wait for the teacher to contact them. Given all the students a teacher is responsible for, when the teacher gets around to having time to make a call, it's usually bad news. Initiating the call early in the school year lets teachers know that you're concerned about your child's education. If your child typically has problems in school, a call early in the year may be your best shot at hearing something positive. When you do hear some good news, make sure you let your child know how important it is. When there are problems, it's time to use Corrective Teaching, or **SODAS**, or to set up a contract.

Whatever the case, calling or meeting with a teacher sends a clear message to everyone (your children, their teachers, the school administration) that you are interested and involved in your children's education.

Using school notes. We usually talk about using a school note when a student is having problems and regular contact between parents and teachers is necessary. It also can be helpful to send a school note when your child is doing well. It gives the teacher and you a chance to praise your child for a job well-done. Likewise, a thank-you note or card can be a nice surprise for your children's teachers. Studies have shown that school notes accompanied by positive and negative consequences have a positive effect on children's school behavior and academic performance.

School notes can be formal or informal. A formal school note can list the child's classes and provide space for the teacher to comment how the child is doing in class or with homework. On a regular basis, the teacher fills out the card and sends it home with the student. Notes can be completed on a daily, weekly, or monthly basis, whichever schedule fits the needs of your child and the teacher.

It helps to keep school note information brief and specific. Typically, teachers don't have the time to fill out lengthy explanations of your child's behavior. Make it easy for the teacher to quickly circle the positive or negative behaviors listed on the note. Have the teacher initial the note or circled items. Ask the teacher to call you if he or she needs to give you more detailed information.

Parents also have found it useful to attach privileges to a child's behavior in school. Parents often write a contract that specifies what their children get to do if they complete the agreed-upon behavior. For example, if your 14-year-old daughter does the assigned homework every day during the week, she gets to go out with friends on Friday night. If she only completes homework four of the five nights, she might only get to have a friend over on Saturday or not go out until she finishes the incomplete homework assignments. See Chapter 13 for more information about contracts.

Some parents want to find out information about their child's classes but don't want the child to carry a note every day. In these cases, an informal school note can be helpful. These usually are written requests for information from the parent to the teacher. These also can be written from the teacher to the parent. In either case, the adults are sharing information about schoolwork or behavior. Often, just letting your children know that you are monitoring their school work can have a positive influence. Whether using formal or informal school notes, it is helpful to make privileges contingent on attending classes, behaving well, and completing homework.

Two examples of school notes are provided on the next page. The first is for younger children or children who have only one teacher each day. The second is for older children or children who have several teachers during their school day. Adapt these examples to work for you.

Working with teachers to solve school problems. To stay involved with your children's education, it helps to attend regularly scheduled meetings with teachers, such as parent-teacher conferences and back-to-school nights.

There also are unscheduled meetings when you get called to the school because of one problem or another. Often, parents are nervous about these types of meetings. We've come up with a list of helpful hints for parents when they get these calls.

Dear Mrs. Maheshwari,

We're trying to help Mahesh do better in school. Please check "Yes" or "No" for each behavior. Then initial and send this note home with Mahesh each day. Thanks.

Mrs. Jageshwari

	M	T	W	T	F
1. Stays in seat	**y/n**	**y/n**	**y/n**	**y/n**	**y/n**
2. Follows directions	**y/n**	**y/n**	**y/n**	**y/n**	**y/n**
3. Turns in homework	**y/n**	**y/n**	**y/n**	**y/n**	**y/n**
Initials	___	___	___	___	___

Teachers,

We are trying to help Mahesh do better in all of his classes. Please note whether Mahesh did these things during this past week and then initial. Please call us at 498-1070 if you have any questions.

Period	Class on Time	Homework Completed	Followed Instructions	Teacher's Initials
1				
2				
3				
4				
5				
6				
7				
8				

- Take time to get calm. Typically, calls about school problems make parents feel anxious, angry, or frustrated. You will be much more likely to help your child solve a problem if you can remain calm and focus on a solution during the meeting with teachers and administrators.
- Find out the exact nature of the problem. Be sure to talk with the teacher or school administrator who is involved with the situation. If they don't explain it clearly, be sure to ask specific questions to help you understand the problem. The focus here is not to challenge whether the problem happened, but to understand what the problem is.
- Ask the teachers or administrators if they have any suggestions for solving the problem or improving the situation. Some teachers and administrators have had a great deal of experience with certain problems. They work with a variety of children and may have effective ways for constructively responding to this particular problem.
- Offer your suggestions for solving the problem or improving the situation. Trust your instincts; no one knows your child as well as you do. Your past experience with your child, both successful and unsuccessful, will help in the development of an effective strategy for solving the problem. Be open to new ideas from the school staff, but also share your opinion about the proposed solution.
- Thank the school staff for their time and concern. Calling a parent to the school is typically stressful for everyone involved. Let the staff know that you appreciate their efforts on behalf of your child.
- Don't take sides or defend your child's behavior. Remember, the goal of the meeting with your child's teacher or school administrator is to get information, solve the immediate problem, and

look for ways to help your child do better in the future. This is neither a time to take sides with the school and complain about your child, nor is it time to take sides with your child and complain about his or her teachers. Work together with the school staff to find an effective solution. Then try your best, and have your child try his or her best, to follow through with the agreed-upon plan.

After the meeting is finished, be sure to talk with your child about the problem and the proposed solution. Keep in touch with the school staff and ask them to do the same with you. Your goal at this point is to help the child learn from the misbehavior and increase the likelihood that the problem will not happen again.

Summary

Children spend a major portion of their waking hours in school. Your involvement and attention to your children's schoolwork are keys to helping them succeed in school. The suggestions in this chapter are based on research studies and our experiences at Boys Town's sites where we provide a home and education for more than a thousand children each year. These are general guidelines and do not cover all of the different types of problems that can occur. If you are experiencing more serious school problems with your child and the suggestions in this chapter don't seem to be improving the situation, then be sure to talk with the school counselor or another professional who can help with your child's particular problems.

If your child has difficulty making the transition from one grade to the next or struggles with the added responsibilities they face each year, the list of suggestions on the following page may be helpful.

Helping Kids Through Transitions in School

School is a series of changes for your children. They move from preschool to elementary to junior high to high school, and then on to a job, vocational school, or college. Each year children must make the transition from summer play to structured school rooms. Every school day, they go from one subject or classroom to another. Here are some hints that parents have shared with us for helping kids through these transitions.

- Be positive about school. Talk with your kids about the good things that happen at school. Tell them about some of your good experiences with school.
- Start talking about school as early in a child's life as possible. Set the expectation that your child will get a good education.
- Expect your child to experience some stress that is related to school, tests, friends, and homework. Be understanding when they tell you about their frustrations.
- Listen to your kids and what they tell you about school. Sometimes it just helps to let them talk about what's going on in their lives. Be supportive and attentive.
- Visit your children's school. Find out about the school day, the administration, and naturally, your children's teachers.
- Praise the good things that your children do. Especially focus on their successful attempts at solving problems.

Notes

Quick Reference

Effective Praise

- Show your approval
- Describe the positive
- Give a reason

Preventive Teaching

- Describe what you would like
- Give a reason
- Practice

Corrective Teaching

- Stop the problem behavior
- Give a consequence
- Describe what you want
- Practice what you want

Teaching Self-Control

Part One: Calming Down

- Describe the problem behavior
- Give clear instructions
- Allow time to calm down

Part Two: Follow-Up Teaching

- Describe what your child could do differently next time
- Practice what your child can do next time
- Give a consequence

Index

C